Coach Johnson,

Thankyou for all you have done for me. I appreciate it so much!
Golf really is a game I can play for the rest of my life.
Thanks for getting me started!

Kate Welsh '06

Golf Digest
American Classic Courses

GOLF'S ENDURING DESIGNS, FROM POT BUNKERS TO ISLAND GREENS

THIS IS A CARLTON BOOK

Distributed by
Andrews McMeel Publishing
4520 Main Street
Kansas City MO 64111 - 7701
(800) 851-8923

10 9 8 7 6 5 4 3 2 1

Text and design copyright © 2003 Carlton Books

GOLF DIGEST is a registered trademark of Advance Magazine Publishers Inc.

A CIP catalogue reference for this book is available from the British Library

ISBN   1 84222 649 5
UPC   8 02880 00028 2

Project Editor: Luke Friend
Project Art Direction: Jim Lockwood
Design: Dominic Baker
Picture Editor: Marc Glanville
Production: Lisa French

Printed and bound in Dubai

Golf Digest

American Classic Courses

GOLF'S ENDURING DESIGNS, FROM POT BUNKERS TO ISLAND GREENS

Contents

Introduction

You can talk about the great challenge of the golf swing all you want, about the quest to discover ways to increase distance and improve accuracy that drives every player regardless of skill, about the incomparable sensation of that one well-struck shot and about how it alone, fleeting though it may be, keeps us coming back to this eternally and infernally frustrating enterprise. But with apologies to Ben Hogan and David Leadbetter and every range rat from West Palm Beach to Tokyo, the game is not the swing.

No, the thing that drives the passion of golf, that elevates it beyond every game known to man, is the one thing that is never the same. Golf is its fields of play, whether set beside rolling ocean or carved from acres of forest. It is what we remember, it is what we extol, it is what we dream about. No matter how repeatable your swing, there is no range on earth that can equal the visual, some would even say spiritual, sensation that comes from stepping to the first tee of a new course, or for that matter stepping on to the 18th green of a favorite old one. It is the incomparable challenge of the game not merely to master the skills required to make a golf swing, but to transport that ability to a venue you could never simulate. But golf's fields of play are so much more than the

simple boundaries in which the contest must take place. At its core, golf is its settings, its backdrops, its landscapes.

Here is a story I remember about the allure of golf's fields of play. Early in my days with golf, a friend and I were in the midst of a long drive that would lead us to one of our favorite golf destinations for a few days away from the daily grind. As the miles rolled by, the anticipation, as anyone who has a passion for this avocation/affliction that is golf knows full well, intensified much like it would for the prospect of setting camp after an epic hike through the Serengeti. We had no intentions of stopping, certainly, hadn't contemplated any outpost where we might pause to stretch our legs. About midway through our journey, we came upon a small sign in

At the great ones, like The Country Club at Brookline, the game's challenge continues to the final green.

Take away the trappings, Augusta National's 13th remains a naturally perfect golf hole.

front of an unpaved stretch of road. The name of the course is lost on me now, but it was adorned with the simple, yet alluring phrase, "Come Play Me!" At the time, I thought it almost silly, but quaint, as if the golf course itself was somehow not only a real living thing, but one that could entice. But there it was calling us back. And so we turned the car around, drove up the dusty road and found ourselves a golf course. We played it, and while nothing dramatic happened—the ghost of Alister Mackenzie didn't approach us from behind the third green, the pro behind the counter didn't turn out to be Old Tom Morris' third cousin, nor was the design itself a lost Donald Ross layout from the early 1920s—what happened was the remarkable experience of

discovery every golf course brings, whether you're playing it for the first time or the hundredth.

Now, of course, I know that golf courses are very much individual entities with personalities and souls and charms often many more times varied than most people you meet. They can be seductive, they can be forgiving, they can be cruel, and they can be inspiring. As living things they change and evolve, and in the best of cases their seductiveness, forgiveness, cruelty and ability to inspire grows, too. That is, I imagine, a good part of what C.B. Macdonald meant when he referred to golf as "Scotland's gift." The pleasure of the physical exercise of playing the game is one thing. That is precisely why multiple-decked driving ranges in Japan are

filled to this day. But the real gift of golf, imported from Scotland, is its riveting environments, created by an intoxicating mixture of art and science, of working with the land and shaping it, of finding holes and of making them work.

Golf course architecture is a mystery, a sort of origami of the landscape, whose methods and theories can be delineated, even taught, but whose actual successful practice is impossible to follow, let alone predict. It comes from some place deeper than topographical maps and blueprint drawings, what one writer once called "walking in the woods and seeing things with your eyes closed that aren't there—yet." Who knows what the requirements are that make an exceptional, visionary golf course architect? George Thomas was a

horticulturist. Donald Ross was a trained carpenter. Alister Mackenzie was a licensed physician. Pete Dye was a successful life insurance salesman. Even Robert Trent Jones Sr., the man most credit with perfecting at least the modern business of golf course architecture, created his own college major on the subject, but even then included in the course such things as history and the classics.

Golf course architecture generally seems only limited by definition. Tom Fazio, perhaps the most celebrated architect of the 1990s, once included this idea of the variety of his projects in his book *Golf Course Designs*. "Each presents a new problem requiring a unique solution and a fresh approach that combines past experience, hard work, knowl-edge, commitment and, above all, a positive attitude... When people ask me to explain how we manage to come up with different designs, my answer is that I have no idea. We just work at it, and we do it."

Perhaps that is as fitting a description as any. What follows in these pages then are living entities that have been created or discovered, but always endlessly worked on by some of the most inventive minds the game has ever known. Anyone who has ever witnessed a golf course come into being must stand in awe at the process of finding and contriving holes from the land. The best courses capture the essence of the game, inspiring and embodying its challenges and torments, its beauty and its mystery.

Are these 50 courses exceptional? No question. These are the courses that are significant not just for their design but for their impact on the game. Many have hosted the most significant championships ever played; others, though, have held nothing much more than a club championship. Certainly, though, there is an individual case for each course featured, whether it be Fishers Island and its profound statement about the work of underappreciated architect Seth Raynor or, on the other end of the spectrum, the incredible blank-slate oasis that is Shadow Creek. Each of these 50 has changed golf in some way and continues to do so.

Choosing 50 golf courses over any other 50 is impossible, of course. It almost makes no logical sense, as judging qual-

The 18th at Shinnecock Hills twists and rolls like an angry, green sea.

Simple, beguiling, beautiful, deadly—the 18th at The Olympic Club is all the best golf can offer.

ity is not a scientific process. But if there is a definitive process for attempting to judge golf courses, it is that employed by *Golf Digest* in its landmark ranking of America's 100 Greatest Courses. It is a process that has certainly evolved over time, but it remains thorough and it stands supreme as the industry standard. Since official rankings started at the magazine in the mid-1960s, some 364 different courses have appeared on its most-desired 100 Greatest list. Literally thousands of other courses have been considered in that time by a panel today that numbers nearly 700.

With that formidable history and process as backdrop, a selection of 50 started first by choosing all the courses that have been featured in every one of the magazine's 19 official

lists since 1966. The remainder of the courses selected for the pages of this book included other significant courses both architecturally and otherwise. In addition, there are 10 courses, each opened since *Golf Digest* first began ranking courses that have been selected under the heading "modern classics." This is an eclectic group that numbers both wonderfully minimalist throwback designs like Sand Hills and the groundbreaking designs like Pete Dye's "stadium golf" treatment at the TPC at Sawgrass. Each of the 50 courses in this book has appeared on the list of America's 100 Greatest Courses several times, an affirmation that the older designs remain steadfastly important today and that the newer designs have elevated themselves beyond any current fad.

Such a list clearly will come under criticism. And there should be an element of joy in that. How for instance can an Inverness or Scioto be chosen over a Beverly or a Holston Hills? How is there room for Peachtree and Spyglass Hill, but not for Hazeltine National? Why not The Prince instead of Mauna Kea, Whistling Straits instead of The Ocean Course, or The Meadow Club instead of Crystal Downs? Those questions are as impossible to answer as they are to find fault with. This sort of debate is not much different than a white paper on the subject of the virtues of one flavor of ice cream over another. The simple fact is, like double chocolate fudge and cherry vanilla, each satisfies according to personal taste.

Let it just be said that this volume includes a collection of vastly American originals whose import and wonder cannot be argued. They are unique, historic and fundamental to the development and experience of the game of golf in America. These are all sources of awe, and they are without question the kinds of places that are full of romance, allure and reward. They are living spiritual things, changing over time and through man's hands, but always inspiring and instilling renewed appreciation of the game.

How such things of beauty and challenge can be found or contrived is a special gift, a gift not even the architect understands sometimes. Michael Hurdzan, a golf course architect for more than 30 years with a Ph.D. in turfgrass science, is

one of the game's current top designers. His grand designs in Canada at Devil's Paintbrush and Devil's Pulpit illustrate in stark contrast the twin themes of creation and discovery that are the hallmarks of exceptional design. Moreover, he is a man of golf with a sense of history (his unmatched personal golf library is testament to that) and a deep understanding both for his craft and the creative process. He knows groundbreaking golf course architecture, but he also knows that even the best architecture comes from some place beyond the hands and minds of man. He knows it cannot be controlled, only ultimately set free.

"There's this story about a woodcarver who was working on a massive oak door," Hurdzan once said. "And he was

carving it in tremendous detail day after day, working on it constantly for a very long time. Finally, his apprentice came to him and asked, 'When will you be finished?' The woodcarver looked at him and just said, 'I'll never be finished with this. Eventually, they'll just come and take it away from me.' "That," said Hurdzan, "is a lot like golf course architecture."

Perhaps the architects never really finished with the courses that follow. Perhaps they also knew they could not keep them from us any longer because we could not wait any longer to play them. Therein lies as good a definition of greatness as there is, namely that the expectation of greatness is fulfilled completely. Here, on these pages, is greatness fulfilled.

Pebble Beach's short 7th hole with its bunkers and other distractions is more challenging than most holes five times its length.

The introduction of Augusta National's famed Amen Corner: the 11th green (left) and par-3 12th.

Augusta National Golf Club

Location: **Augusta, Georgia**
Opened: **1934**
Architect: **Alister Mackenzie & Bobby Jones**
Par: **72**
Length: **7,290 yards**

There is no golf course in the world that shines more dramatically in the mind's eye of the average golfer than Augusta National Golf Club. Largely, this is to do with its annual appearance on television each April for the Masters Tournament. Just as the tournament often seems to demand perfection in the play of its participants, the golf course remains an example of near perfection in design.

Though it has changed, the soul of the golf course existed long before there were tournaments, maybe long before there was even a golf course on the property. The site had an immediate impact on the course's founder, Bobby Jones.

"Perfect!" Jones said when he first saw the property laid out before him on a tour of the grounds in 1931. "And to think this ground has been lying here all these years waiting for someone to come along and lay a course on it."

Set on what was once an indigo plantation and later a tree nursery, the Augusta National emerged through the work of Alister Mackenzie and Jones himself. As Herbert Warren Wind once wrote, "Jones and Mackenzie agreed on the value of creating holes that were scenically arresting as well as functionally sound." The result may have been the consummate example of the philosophy of strategic design. There are options everywhere here, whether it be in how much one challenges a fairway bunker or how aggressive a play to make toward the flag or even how creative one chooses to be when playing shots just off or on the greens. Even though the course has been tinkered with over the years, relocating the 10th green one year, redesigning the par-3 16th another, and so on, its fundamental nature has never changed.

It is the game's great cathedral, displaying at once the magical intricacy of a Notre Dame and the sheer emotional power of a Taj Mahal. And yet despite the beauty of the place, the stately pines, the glorious pinks and reds of its azaleas in bloom, and even the almost blindingly white sand in its bunkers, it is still, first and foremost, a complete challenge as a golf course. That is no doubt one reason why the game's greatest players have routinely triumphed there with Jack Nicklaus winning six times, Arnold Palmer four, and Nick Faldo, Gary Player, Sam Snead, Jimmy Demaret and Tiger Woods three each.

What Jones and Mackenzie combined to produce and what was continued later with the help of other noteworthy architects such as Perry Maxwell, Robert Trent Jones Sr., George Cobb, Jack Nicklaus and Tom Fazio was a design that reflected Jones's wish that the course be "eminently playable from the regular tees for the medium- and high-handicap golfer while simultaneously presenting a stiff examination from the back tees for the low-handicap or scratch golfer." They did this with subtlety, always present-ing the player with at least a moment of uncertainty, first on the tee as he considered his options and then in the fairway where its carefully preserved or contrived contours invite disquiet. Its greens are not merely difficult to hit, but a challenge to hit in precisely the right spots. As for its best holes, clearly the back nine has gained favor for its relentless drama, highlighted by the early triumvirate of Amen Corner—the brutish 11th, the delicately devilish par-3 12th and the strategic par-5 13th—where all three holes are intruded upon by Rae's Creek. But ultimately Augusta National is so much more than its highlights, it is a symphony full of fantastic intrigue and overwhelming majesty. As Nicklaus once said, it is "one of the most testing and interesting inland courses in the world, strategic golf at its finest."

1934: First Masters tournament, then known as the Augusta National Invitation, is won by Horton Smith.

1954: Sam Snead defeats Ben Hogan in a playoff to win Masters.

1958: Arnold Palmer wins his first Masters.

1963: Jack Nicklaus wins his first Masters.

1996: Nick Faldo wins his third Masters, rallying from a six-stroke deficit to overtake Greg Norman.

1997: 21-year-old Tiger Woods sets the Masters scoring record in winning his first major championship by 12 strokes.

DEFINING MOMENTS

1986: Nicklaus wins his record-breaking sixth title, shooting a back-nine 30 to become the oldest Masters winner at age 46.

2001: Nearly 300 yards is added to the overall length of the course as nine holes are changed to varying degrees.

2002: Tiger Woods wins his third Masters title.

The 10th hole, whose original green was by the bunker in the distance, drops more than 100 feet from tee to green.

Feature Hole

13

Bobby Jones had general disdain for long par-5 holes, "Here," he said, "you don't start playing golf until your third shot." The 13th hole, a prototypical Jones par four-and-a-half, was the first hole he and Alister Mackenzie saw when they toured the property. Set in a natural sloping field with a tributary of Rae's Creek guarding both the left side of the fairway and the front of the green, the 13th was judged by *Golf Digest* to be the best par 5 in America. The ideal line off the tee is close to the edge of the creek with a long drive, which gives a typical player a flatter lie and an excellent opportunity to reach the green in two shots. The challenge is increased by the multitiered green and exacerbated by a nettlesome swale behind it. "In my opinion," Jones later wrote in his autobiography, "this 13th hole is one of the finest holes for competitive play I have ever seen."

510 YARDS

PAR 5

Baltusrol Golf Club (Lower)

Location: **Springfield, New Jersey**
Opened: **1895**
Architects: **A.W. Tillinghast/Robert Trent Jones Sr.**
Par: **72**
Length: **7,221 yards**

A s some have suggested, to look at the Lower Course at Baltusrol Golf Club is not to see much. Indeed, *Golf Digest* once headlined a preview of the golf course for the 1993 U.S. Open as "The Longest Yawn." But then you look at its history and the glaring truth stands out: There have been a record seven U.S. Opens played at the club, and Jack Nicklaus won two of them. That should tell you something about the strength of this storied layout.

Originally the work of A.W. Tillinghast and then refortified by Robert Trent Jones Sr., Baltusrol symbolizes the definitive requirements for a U.S. Open-style golf course: parkland, deep bunkering, heavy rough, fast greens and plenty of length. It is a course that forces precision off the tee, as bunkers blemish the landscape in all the right places. But Baltusrol does not overstate its case. According to Rees Jones, a great Baltusrol fan who also did some modernization work on his father's tinkering in the early 1990s, the strength of Baltusrol Lower lies in its relatively unadorned presentation: "I love it because it is not overdone and everything works. It lulls you to sleep because it doesn't look as hard as it really is."

The apparent sameness, though, is interrupted with anything but boring challenges, like those at No. 8 with its pearshaped green and the disorienting bunker well short of the green, or at No. 11, a sharp dogleg gouged by eight different bunkers lining the fairway and encircling the green. For some, it is the 13th hole that stands out with its troubling creek that once cost Bobby Jones a U.S. Amateur victory. And the back-to-back par-5 finish is as much a mental marathon as a physical endurance test.

There are 126 bunkers on the Lower Course, positioned to the left and right of the fairway in the landing area. Around the greens, however, they often do not directly block the entrance to a green, only on the short holes or when a

The 630-yard 17th hole gets harder and tighter the farther it goes.

player is expected to have a lofted shot into a hole location. But that was typical Tillie. "I think that I will always adhere to my old theory that a controlled shot to a closely guarded green is the surest test of any man's golf," he once wrote. But Tillinghast's bunkers were both hazard and artistic effect. As Rees Jones says of Tillinghast: "He was the first architect who really worked at creating beauty in his bunkers."

Of course, there was an element of wickedness in those bunkers, and they play a role in Baltusrol's closing stretch. Indeed, legendary champion Bobby Jones once called the 18th hole one of the strongest finishes in golf. The back-to-back par 5s to end the round include the once-thought-to-be-unreachable 17th hole that was stretched to 630 yards for the 1993 U.S. Open. Of course, long hitter John Daly landed his second shot—a 1-iron from 295 yards—on the green during the Open. The 17th is split by a one-time Sahara bunker that has since been converted to a collection of cluster-bomb traps. On 18, the challenge lies in trying to go at a green with a long iron from a downhill lie. More than reachable for many players, the seeds of doubt are spread, though, by the six bunkers fronting the green.

The long uphill walk to the 18th green symbolizes the endurance test that is Baltusrol's Lower Course. Its challenge isn't merely physical, it wears on even those with the strongest will. Rees Jones thinks Tillinghast would still recognize his design despite the changes:

"In Baltusrol, Tillinghast left the world a golf course that has multiple shot options, one which requires a premeditated strategy. Baltusrol is different from the golf course that Tillinghast opened in the 1920s, but it doesn't feel that way."

Feature Hole

4

You can focus on other more crucial elements of Baltusrol's Lower Course, more important late-round holes, but you simply cannot ignore the photogenic quality of the first par 3 on the course. Of course, it also has the best story of an architect making his point of any hole in the history of golf. Robert Trent Jones Sr. added a longer tee to the hole that plays over a large pond. When several Baltusrol officials voiced their concern to the great architect that the hole was patently unfair, Jones simply answered their complaints with the swing of a 4-iron. Fetching a club from one of his assistants, Jones went to the tee and laced a shot right at the pin, the ball landed six feet away and then gently trickled into the hole for an ace. Said Jones calmly, "Gentlemen, I think the hole is eminently fair."

195 YARDS PAR 3

The 3rd hole is a 466-yard dogleg and not any easier because it plays downhill.

1954: Unheralded Ed Furgol, plays an escape shot on the final hole up a parallel fairway from the 18th hole of the Upper Course, and wins the U.S. Open by one shot, sinking a six-foot putt on the final hole to secure the victory.

1961: Mickey Wright dominates the final day of the U.S. Women's Open, shooting 138 in the final two rounds to win by six shots.

1980: Having not won a tournament in the preceding year (for the first time in his career), Jack Nicklaus returns to the stage in dramatic fashion, winning the U.S. Open and setting a new all-time scoring record of 272.

DEFINING
MOMENTS

1993: Lee Janzen outduels Payne Stewart over the final 18 holes to win the 93rd U.S. Open. Janzen equals Nicklaus' scoring record, thanks to a chip-in birdie on the 16th hole and a closing four on the 18th.

The par–5 6th works around a lake from start to finish; John Daly once made an 18 here.

Bay Hill Club

Location: **Orlando, Florida**
Opened: **1961**
Architects: **Dick Wilson/Arnold Palmer & Ed Seay**
Par: **72**
Length: **7,239 yards**

As Arnold Palmer tells it in his autobiography, *A Golfer's Life*, the first time he saw Bay Hill in 1965, he told his wife, Winnie, he wanted to buy the place lock, stock and barrel. It took about a decade before Palmer could close on the club, but eventually he did buy it. Ever since, he's gone about making it his own.

Bay Hill was originally a Dick Wilson design on rolling property with a somewhat substantial elevation change for the typically flat land of central Florida. Palmer, the architect, along with his right-hand man Ed Seay, re-made the course in the image of Palmer, the player. For the most part, the routing is essentially the same. Length has been added, holes have been converted from par 4s to par 5s, and the other way around. But mostly today, it has become the ultimate example of Palmer's philosophy of golf; it is bold here, brash there, it has a swagger to it at nearly every turn. This is a course where the driver is demanded and rewarded, where the aggressive line comes with a great upside but with a potentially nightmarish downside, too, and where the hero almost always wins the day. Bay Hill is John Wayne, James Bond and Indiana Jones. Bay Hill is Arnold Palmer.

The tone, that Bay Hill will not be a leisurely stroll, is set relatively early: The course opens with a 441-yard par 4, changed from a leisurely par-5 starter, continues with a 218-yard par 3 to a green fronted by bunkers and a 395-yard par 4 that rings around the largest lake on the property. And then comes the chance to make up some ground on a par 5.

This is how the whole round measures up at Bay Hill. A series of demanding holes, followed by a chance to make up ground on the par 5s or the occasional short par 4. One of those potential makeup par 5s is anything but a pushover. The 558-yard sixth moves counterclockwise around the same lake players first saw at the third. The temptation is to go at the 47-yard deep green with two big hits. The risk does not always pay off, however. Jim Colbert once made a nine there. Lee Trevino posted an 11 and even Palmer himself once wrote down a 10. All took a backseat to the 18 recorded by John Daly at this hole in the final round of the 1998 Bay Hill Invitational.

Water is part of the action on 10 holes at Bay Hill, but true to his charging nature, the King saved his master strokes for the end. His first change was to make the 18th hole a heroic par 4 instead of a routine par 5 by bringing the green closer to the water's edge and later ringing its border with rocks. The 16th, meanwhile, was later converted from a dullish par 4 to a gambler's par 5 with water, bunkers and a wickedly sloping green all weighing on the player's mind. And while the only substantial changes to 17 have been added length, it remains one of Palmer's favorite par 3s in the game. And one of the most unrelenting.

Still, for all the danger at Bay Hill's finish, it has made for great drama in the final rounds of Palmer's own PGA Tour event every March, the Bay Hill Invitational. Routinely, the 16th hole provides the most sudden turnarounds among the leaders as sevens are nearly as likely as threes. No. 17 is a hold-on par 3 that almost never yields a birdie. And 18 provides the most excitement. But the best players love what Palmer has created. Pressure and possibility are Bay Hill's calling cards, says Tiger Woods. "It's very similar to when you are playing down the stretch in a major championship. Anything can happen and it's so easy to make a bogey."

Or, he could have added, a birdie. Which is just the way the King wants it.

1965: Arnold Palmer plays an exhibition match at Bay Hill with Jack Nicklaus, Dave Ragan and Don Cherry. Enthralled with the course, he immediately sets in motion plans to purchase the development.

1989: Among the changes instituted by Palmer for the 1990 tournament is the pivotal switching of the 16th hole from a par 4 to a par 5.

DEFINING MOMENTS

1979: In preparation for the Florida Citrus Open moving to his course at Bay Hill, Palmer converts the 18th hole to a meaty, demanding par 4.

2002: Tiger Woods wins for the third time in a row at Bay Hill, becoming the first player ever to do that at Palmer's tournament.

Feature Hole

Both the 18th hole and the first hole at Bay Hill play at 441 yards. The similarity ends there. No. 1 is a fine opener, but as a finish, Palmer's redesigned 18th is fit for a King. While the fairway is wide, the best angle to the green is up the left side, the same side, of course, as the out-of-bounds fence. From there, players must hit a large, narrow green at the edge of a giant lake. Palmer brought this green down to the level of the lake as one of his first moves, and it has resulted in some spectacular finishes, like when Robert Gamez holed a 7-iron from the middle of the fairway for an eagle to win the 1990 tournament. In 2001, Tiger Woods feathered a 5-iron from the hardpan left of the 18th fairway onto the green and then won the tournament with a birdie to a roar usually reserved for the tournament host.

441 YARDS PAR 4

One of Arnie's favorites, the par–3 17th plays even harder than it looks.

Bellerive Country Club

Location: **St. Louis, Missouri**
Opened: **1960**
Architect: **Robert Trent Jones Sr.**
Par: **72**
Length: **7,503 yards**

Subtlety was never Robert Trent Jones Sr.'s strong suit, at least not in terms of golf course architecture. When his courses were tagged with the catchphrase "hard par, easy bogey," it wasn't an exercise in semantics; it was the law. And nowhere was the law more stringently upheld than at Bellerive Country Club, a host site for two major championships, and a course about as subtle as a cinder block—and nearly as impenetrable.

Bellerive Country Club had been a fixture in St. Louis for decades, first opening a nine-hole course in 1897. In the late 1950s, though, its members sought more space and a new golf course. They turned to Trent Jones, a man who more or less invented the modern business of golf course architecture while at the same time gaining a reputation for building "championship-style" layouts. It is an ambiguous, or at least arbitrary, phrase, but to Jones' way of thinking, a championship layout meant one thing: a golf course with what he called "character." This place, Jones said, had that element: "Bellerive's rough hills, its creeks and its wooded slopes were the ingredients needed to design a truly championship course."

Jones used those ingredients merely to accent a golf course that would be long, hard, unrelenting, and not necessarily everyone's favorite.

Dan Jenkins once suggested Jones may have gone too far. "Robert Trent Jones courses are always famed for their length and boredom. This course was so long and boring it makes you wonder how Jones could have ever been in fashion."

But in truth Bellerive was Jones at the height of his heroic-style architecture powers. His hallmarks are at every turn: extraordinarily long tee boxes that somehow make every hole seem narrower, large fairway bunkers that subdue nearly every aggressive desire on the tee, and city-block-sized, multi-level greens (they average nearly 9,000 square feet)

The par–5 17th is long; water makes it brutal.

that make pins as easy to locate as missing persons. No wonder players started calling it the Green Monster.

"It's a very good driving course," said Nick Price, who won the PGA Championship there in 1992, the first of his three major titles. "And you have to be very specific with distances and accuracy with your iron play, or you can leave yourself with some very difficult, long putts."

Given a blank slate and unencumbered by housing or other property issues, Jones constructed 18 rounds of repeating blows to the solar plexus. The day opens and closes with long par 4s, including a classic finishing hole with a green fronted by huge amoeba-like bunkers, forcing a high, soft, precise final full swing of the day. The closing stretch of holes 16, 17, 18 reads 230, 604 and 457 on the scorecard.

Jones anticipated how the American game was changing to an aerial assault. To force the issue, he wanted players to hit a driver, and he wanted their approach shots to have to carry all the way to the green. Anything struck off line from the tee would encounter deep rough or sand or perhaps a pond, any approach shot less than solidly hit would fall short into a sloping bunker, or worse, water. In short, no fun.

Nevertheless, the value of Jones's design at Bellerive was proven by its major championship winners. In addition to Price's win at the PGA in 1992, a gritty Gary Player won the U.S. Open in 1965 to earn the career Grand Slam. In each case, the relentlessness of Bellerive—and Jones—emerged as the ultimate winner. For Jones, it was all in a day's work. "This course, as I sought to make it, is one of the great courses in the United States," he said. "I have built a lot of courses, and Bellerive is one of the best."

Feature Hole

18

This is the epitome of the classic par-4 finishing hole, Robert Trent Jones-style. Players are asked to gun a driver out of a claustrophobic chute of trees to a fairway splotched by a 30-yard-long ink-blot bunker bumping against the left corner of the dogleg. Successfully challenging the fairway bunker requires a drive that carries nearly 290 yards. Should a player favor the safer route on the right side of the fairway, he'll most likely face a second shot that must clear two bunkers clustered in the front right side of a green that slopes significantly from right to left. Gary Player remembers telling himself at the 72nd hole of his U.S. Open win there in 1965, "You've wanted to win the U.S. Open all your life, so let's get up there and bust this thing right down the middle." Player made his par to force an 18-hole playoff, which he won handily the next day.

454 YARDS

PAR 4

There is very little bailout room at Bellerive's par-3 3rd hole.

1960: Course opens and shortly after an agreement is signed that it will serve as host site for the 1965 U.S. Open.

1981: Jim Holtgrieve, a St. Louis native, wins the first-ever U.S. Mid-Amateur championship, defeating fellow Walker Cupper Bob Lewis 2-up in the final.

DEFINING MOMENTS

1965: Gary Player wins the U.S. Open in an 18-hole playoff over Kel Nagle.

1992: Nick Price's final round of 70 vaults him to the top of the leaderboard to secure a three-stroke victory in the PGA Championship.

Bethpage State Park (Black)

Location: **Farmingdale, New York**
Opened: **1936**
Architect: **Joseph Burbeck/A.W. Tillinghast**
Par: **71**
Length: **7,297 yards**

Despite its reputation for excess, golf in America still has a decidedly proletarian air. Simply put, the overwhelming majority of the golf played in this country is played by golfers at courses open to the public. Among that list, there is no more public place to play golf than New York's Bethpage State Park on Long Island, what legendary New York master planner Robert Moses once called "the People's Country Club." And if that everyman's enclave has a prized possession, it is the revered Black Course, a golf experience so overwhelming it comes with its own stop sign. "Warning," reads a placard on a gate by the first tee. "The Black Course is an extremely difficult course which is recommended only for highly skilled golfers."

This is not an idle threat. The Black Course is epic stuff: it traverses seven miles and climbs nine separate hills. Tees are elevated, and greens are elevated, sometimes even on the same hole, notably the 18th. And, of course, there is the lasting impression of the humongous Bethpage bunkers, filled with more than 8,000 tons of sand, stretching out as long as football fields and as wide as basketball courts.

The initial plan was to make it hard in a first-class way. The huge deposits of sandy soil on the site got both architect-consultant A.W. Tillinghast and on-site architect-builder Joseph Burbeck thinking of turning the Black into a public Pine Valley. So the Black Course rolls along like the sea in a tsunami, its directions nearly as predictable. While the first hole swings to the right, the second hole goes left, and then the fourth hole climbs in a series of ridges from tee to green. And all this before the course starts to get difficult.

The Black Course, with its elevation and scarring bunkers, is very much an aerial assault experience, not unlike another Tillinghast stronghold, Winged Foot Golf Club's West Course. There, Tillinghast's marching orders were to produce "a man-sized course." Well, at Bethpage Black,

Architect Rees Jones enhanced the 18th hole's difficulty with beefed up bunkers, making it fit the rest of the course.

Tillinghast built a working-man-sized course. It is brash and bullying and rough around the edges. When Rees Jones was brought in to prepare the course for the 2002 U.S. Open, he took the epic scale of Bethpage and enhanced it, making it bigger and bolder without losing its subtlety.

The key is, of course, the mastodon-sized bunkers. Starting with the fourth hole, the bunkers become bigger elements in the landscape. There are dramatic cross bunkers set on diagonals on the par-5 fourth, the par-4 fifth and the long seventh, which plays as a par 5 for regular Joes but is a par 4 for the big games.

Lost in the shuffle perhaps are the flattish greens, a concession some say to the average golfer's ability level and the rest of the course's demands. But others disagree, like Sergio Garcia, who first experienced the greens at the 2002 U.S. Open. "I think these greens are the slopiest, flattest greens I've ever seen in my life," he said then.

The bunkers become dramatic window dressing again at the 10th and 11th, the only parallel holes on the course. Here, a stretch of wild mounds and five herculean bunkers divide the two fairways.

The finishing four holes offer little relaxation either, especially the uphill approach to the 15th, the toughest green on the course. Jones' masterful retrofitting of the 18th, with the addition of pinching bunkers (nine of them), mounds and fescue framing the landing area, provides a final hurdle.

The Black is a source of pride to the regulars who sleep in their cars or hang on the telephone line hoping to secure a weekend tee time. It may be called the People's Country Club, but there is nothing commonplace about it.

分析

1940: Despite referring to the Black Course as "an unfair test of golf," Sam Snead shoots a course-record 70 and defeats Byron Nelson one-up in an exhibition match.

1995: The U.S. Golf Association inspect the Black Course as a potential U.S. Open site. The course plays to rave reviews and is selected to play host to the 2002 U.S. Open, the first truly publicly owned facility to do so.

DEFINING **MOMENTS**

1972: Mal Galletta Jr. posts a bogey-free 65 to set the all-time competitive course record. The mark is equalled four times, including by Rick Hartmann in 2001 at the Met Open at the freshly refurbished course.

2002: Tiger Woods wins the U.S. Open at the longest U.S. Open course in history. Woods is the only player to finish under par for the tournament with a four-day total of 277, three shots clear of Phil Mickelson.

The shelf that houses the green on the par–3 third is not always receptive.

Feature Hole

After the grand slog that is Bethpage Black's back nine (four par 4s longer than 450 yards), it may come as a surprise to think that the par-3 17th is the toughest hole on the inward nine. Until you step to the tee and see it. Or, more accurately, don't see it. The long par 3 is so heavily bunkered that there almost appears to be no green to aim for. Three jarring bunkers with faces upturned guard the front of the putting surface like nightclub bouncers. More consternating is how long misses can find their way to a tiny bunker behind the thin green, which actually angles away from the golfer slightly and is just 13 yards deep at the center of the green. A ridge runs through the middle of the green, separating the putting surface into two targets and making for some wild putts if your aim is off.

213 YARDS

PAR 3

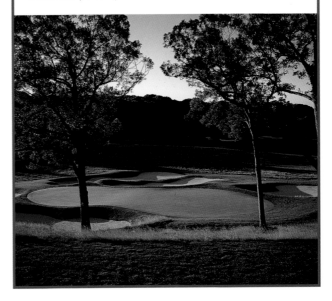

Chicago Golf Club

Location: **Wheaton, Ilinois**
Opened: **1894/1923**
Architect: **C.B. Macdonald/Seth Raynor**
Par: **70**
Length: **6,574 yards**

Though it was the irrepressible C.B. Macdonald who did the original layout at Chicago Golf Club, it is his understudy Seth Raynor's work that exists today as one of the great examples of classic golf course architecture. Of course, it was Macdonald's ideas that Raynor so carefully constructed into reality. As a result, Chicago Golf Club serves as both a museum piece and a worthy examination of all the skills required of the best players.

Because Chicago Golf Club's roots lie with Macdonald, whose fascination with the game developed while he was studying abroad in Scotland at St. Andrews University, it is a real bridge between what architecture was in the Old Country and what it could be in the New. Although Raynor was responsible for the on-site particulars in 1922–23, he was clearly trained at the foot of the master. Said C.B. Macdonald in a letter to the club prior to Raynor's arrival; "You may rest assured Mr. Raynor will go out with a free mind. He naturally has absorbed my ideas of golf architecture, as he has done all the work for me during the last 10 years, and so far as I know there are no golf courses in the country that compare with his."

Their combined efforts clearly reflect the influence that the great courses of St. Andrews had on Macdonald. Pot bunkers appear in the most gruesome places, greenside sand is occasionally 10 feet below the putting surface and the squareish greens themselves are epic in size, challenging the player's skill at lag putting. Perhaps this is why legendary putter Ben Crenshaw finds Chicago Golf Club to be one of his favorites, even going so far as to join the club himself.

Chicago Golf Club, the first 18-hole course in America and one of the original five clubs that founded what would become the United States Golf Association, was instrumental in the early championship history of golf in America. It was the host site for eight U.S. championships from 1897

The angling 16th is one of only two par–5s at Chicago Golf Club.

until 1912: four U.S. Amateurs, three U.S. Opens, and a U.S. Women's Amateur.

Certainly shortish by modern standards, Chicago Golf Club demands an efficiency of purpose that goes well beyond the grip-it-and-rip-it mentality. Its layout is more links-like than parkland, though the nearest ocean might be about a thousand miles away. Located a half hour or so southwest of the city of Chicago, it cannot even boast of being on the edge of a Great Lake. But it feels the winds of its namesake city, and is designed accordingly.

While clumps of trees dot the property, they rarely significantly disturb play. Still, stray from the fairway and you find yourself in tall, reddish brown prairie fescue. Long bunkers cut into driving areas at rakish angles, daring the bold driver to fly over them. This, of course, is pure Macdonald,

who once explained his aggressive approach to course design as follows, "This helps to make a man know and study his limitations and, if he is inclined to conceit, he will find his niblick has drawn a hard day's work."

Chicago Golf Club is ultimately a straightforward-looking course riddled with options that become increasingly defined as a player's skills develop. There are tributes to the great holes of Scotland, like the Redan-style par-3 sixth, the punch-bowl green at the 12th and even a copy of sorts of the famed Principal's Nose bunker on the Old Course at St. Andrews. But even so, Chicago Golf Club remains an American original. As Crenshaw once wrote in the club's centennial history book in 1992, "Nearly all of the holes at Chicago Golf Club have one outstanding feature that makes the playing experience unique."

Feature Hole

True to the nature of C.B. Macdonald, the bunkering at the 12th hole is relatively insidious. Riveted with six bunkers placed in all the right places, including a pot bunker that haunts the middle of the fairway short of the green, the 12th calls for a careful drive down the left to give a proper angle to the diagonal punch-bowl-style green. This hole clearly illustrates how Raynor and MacDonald wanted doubt to enter a player's mind as he stepped onto the tee because trouble exists in varying degrees on both sides of the fairway, and one misplayed shot from tee brings other hazards into play. As Ben Crenshaw once noted of the 12th, "This hole is gorgeous in the late afternoon, when its very nature casts the shadows of many contours."

414 YARDS

PAR 4

At the 15th green and elsewhere, the distinctive clubhouse stands watch.

1892: C.B. Macdonald original nine holes are designed; second nine added a year later.

1894: C.B. Macdonald designs the full 18 holes at the present site in Wheaton, Ill.

1897: Host site for jointly conducted U.S. Open, won by Joe Lloyd, and U.S. Amateur, won by H.J. Whigham.

1900: Harry Vardon wins by two strokes over J.H. Taylor to claim U.S. Open.

1979: U.S. Senior Amateur is held and is won by William C. Campbell.

DEFINING MOMENTS

1923: Macdonald's partner, Seth Raynor, completes redesign of course.

1928: Captained by Bobby Jones, U.S. defeats Great Britain and Ireland in the Walker Cup, 11–1.

1997: USGA announces that the 2005 Walker Cup will return to Chicago. "The course is as good today as when Charles Blair Macdonald designed it," says F. Morgan Taylor Jr., chairman of the USGA Championship Committee.

Colonial Country Club

Location: **Fort Worth, Texas**	
Opened: **1936**	
Architect: **John Bredemus/Perry Maxwell**	
Par: **70**	
Length: **7,080 yards**	

T he vision for a great golf course lies within the creative mind of a golf course architect, but the energy, the sustaining force that makes a great course not merely a possibility but an eventuality, comes from another man seized with the passion of to make greatness happen. It was true of Bobby Jones' confidant Clifford Roberts at Augusta National, of Samuel F.B. Morse at Pebble Beach and for the Texas jewel that is Colonial Country Club it was personified in founder and life force Marvin Leonard.

Leonard's success in business and his desire to bring bentgrass greens to Texas led him to develop Colonial in the mid-1930s in the southwest section of Fort Worth. According to the club's official history, Leonard sought plans from architects Perry Maxwell and John Bredemus early on, asking them both to submit five separate routings. Once he had received these, he called for five more from each man. Though he settled on Bredemus, Leonard would bring in Maxwell to strengthen the course in preparation for the 1941 U.S. Open. What Leonard ultimately desired was a course fit for championship play and that is what he got. It is a big-hearted test fit for the persona of its home state.

Colonial with its firm, fast conditions, ever-present wind and narrow fairways bordered by trees and the Clear Fork of the Trinity River asks for a mixture of control and power at every turn. And it hits you hard early. The trio of holes three through five are known as "the Horrible Horseshoe," and feature two par 4s of more than 470 yards and a par 3 of nearly 250 yards. Truly, though, these words apply equally to every corner of the golf course. Throughout its layout, Colonial boasts a seemingly never-ending supply of tight squeezes, with more than the occasional pecan tree or oak hanging over this fairway or that green. And its back nine is a relentless anvil chorus: aside from the two par 3s, both of which involve water, the shortest hole is 383 yards. More

Though the 14th at Colonial turns left, a tee shot slightly right can be blocked, too.

than one champion has called it as tough a course as is played in golf. Its requirements were simple. "The tee ball is vital here," said Billy Casper, champion in 1964. "You've got to get the ball out there in a good spot so you've got a chance on your second. And this is on every hole. Of course, the approaches are tough, too, but if you don't keep it in play off the tee, you're dead here."

Curtis Strange, even though he never won here, remained enthralled. "It's one of the great golf courses of the world," he said. "Why can't they build them like this today?"

Within its first five years of existence, Colonial was the site for the U.S. Open and would later serve as the home of the PGA Tour's Colonial National Invitation tournament every year, beginning in 1946. That tournament saw the greatest players win, including Jack Nicklaus, Arnold Palmer, Billy Casper, Lee Trevino, Tom Watson, Ben Crenshaw and Sam Snead, but none greater than Ben Hogan, who won at Colonial five times from 1946–59.

Colonial, which came to be known as "Hogan's Alley," has been altered slightly over the years by both nature and man, including an unsuccessful, and short-lived, effort by Hogan in 1968. However, its demands have not been softened, despite the once-held mantra of older members who would proudly announce to first-timers, "If you think the course is tough now, you should have seen it before the river tore it up." Holes move both ways, and more often than not a shot that does not intentionally bend will wind up off the fairway or green, in a bunker, a ditch or the river. Said Hogan, "A straight ball will get you in more trouble at Colonial than any course I know."

1941: After updating his golf course, owner Marvin Leonard conducts a successful U.S. Open, the first time the U.S. Open has ever been held in the Southwest. Craig Wood wins with a four-round total of four-over 284.

1949: Ben Hogan, recuperating at home in Fort Worth, plays his first 18-hole round in 11 months after being severely injured in an auto accident. Six months later he wins the U.S. Open.

1953: Hogan wins the Colonial National Invitational Tournament for the fourth time and for the second time back-to-back.

1991: Colonial plays host to the U.S. Women's Open, where Meg Mallon's final-round 67 in scorching 100-degree heat give her a two-stroke victory and a one-under total of 283.

DEFINING MOMENTS

1998: Tom Watson wins for the first time at Colonial and for what would turn out to be the final time on the regular tour, posting four rounds in the 60s to win by two shots.

You can't be too precise at the short par–4 17th.

Feature Hole

The fifth exemplifies the combination of power and precision demanded by Colonial. One of the three holes built by Perry Maxwell specifically for the 1941 U.S. Open, the hole is lined by mammoth pecan trees and the Trinity River, which swings along the entire right side of the hole. Arnold Palmer once said, "I consider it a great hole because sooner or later you must play a difficult shot." Others were not so diplomatic, including 1951 Colonial National Invitation champion Cary Middlecoff, who was only partly kidding when he once suggested the hole was so difficult it made him throw up. The hole can be nearly unplayable from anywhere other than the left-center of the fairway, but the prevailing wind pushes shots toward the river, and the two-tiered green is pinched by bunkers in three places. It's easy to see why they call No. 5 "Death Valley."

470 YARDS

PAR 4

Crystal Downs Country Club

Location: **Frankfort, Michigan**
Opened: **1932**
Architect: **Alister Mackenzie/Perry Maxwell**
Par: **70**
Length: **6,518 yards**

In these days of mass communication where television and other media relay images of every kind to any place instantly and where getting from here to anywhere is no more difficult than imagining it, the idea that there may still be places of uncompromised value hidden from the general public view seems impossible to believe. And then you are presented with a truly inventive, truly special escape like Crystal Downs. Under-appreciated by the masses for at least its first half-century of existence, this Alister Mackenzie-Perry Maxwell masterstroke is sparkling evidence of the limitless allure of the game of golf and its playing fields.

Mackenzie, who was making his way back across America with the intention of returning home to Scotland, along with his then associate Maxwell, was talked into a trip to the wilds of Northern Michigan. What they saw once they got to this pristine golfing land set on a 100-foot-high sand-ridge overlooking both Crystal Lake and Lake Michigan was an opportunity to work a magical piece of property.

Mackenzie would draw up the holes in the late 1920s, not long after finishing his work at Cypress Point and his touch-up work at Pebble Beach, and only a few years before his collaboration with Bobby Jones at Augusta National. Clearly at the height of his game, he created at Crystal Downs a series of unconventional but spectacular holes (the kidney-shaped green on the seventh hole is unforgettable), all of them legitimate challenges for even players of the highest ability both then and now. The combination of the setting, the ever-present wind off Lake Michigan, the staggered, undulating, angled fairways and the adventurous greens make Crystal Downs a unique challenge.

From the opening tee shot, a goodly measure of the front nine lies before the golfer, and while it is a view to be savored, it comes not without a good measure of fear. The opener plays a stern 460 yards into the prevailing wind and

The 9th hole may have been an afterthought but playing it requires your full attention.

on every side the miss area is lined with unkempt fescue. The layout's features and strengths are uncommonly superior, whether it's the inventive, complex green at No. 7 or the wickedly penal bunkering of the so-called scabs at No. 6 or the six-foot, back-to-front slopes on greens like No. 2.

Mackenzie and Maxwell infused an otherwise shortish layout with plenty of depth and breadth of challenge. Only about 6,500 yards long, there are still four par 4s that measure at least 425 yards, four that measure less than 360 yards and two legitimate three-shot par 5s. But there was a calculus to the layout, as the shortest par 4s were routinely galvanized with the wildest greens, while those holes that demanded more with the longer clubs were less taxing once the putting surface was reached. Holes that run downhill might more often than not play into the prevailing breeze, while the uphill shots might be downwind. Equally impressive is the bunkering here, at once intricate and ghastly, as at holes six, seven and 18, but always the game reverts to the greens, a perfect testament to the intimidating undulations dubbed "Maxwell Rolls." At Crystal Downs putts routinely run into bunkers or back down the fairway.

In the end, Crystal Downs is that perfect meeting of an enthralling site with a pair of great golf minds at their most inventive. It exemplifies at every turn three of Mackenzie's famed 13 Rules, namely that "every hole should have a different character," that "there should be an infinite variety of strokes required to play the various holes," and that "the course should be so interesting that even the plus man is constantly stimulated to improve his game in attempting shots he had hitherto been unable to play."

Feature Hole

17

Crystal Downs is universally credited with its wickedly good short par 4s (the wild variety of options on the 353-yard fifth and the almost L-shaped but completely puttable green on No. 7 certainly stand out), and the 17th is a fine example of the subtle challenge that can be found on a hole that barely plays 300 yards. It is full of distractions. The fairway rolls like the sea in a storm and it is quite normal for the hole to play straight into a stiff breeze. A chute of trees demands a solid, sure strike off the tee. Amid all this you need to position the ball off the tee both to find a flat area in the fairway and to be able to attack the green from the proper angle. There may be sanctuary in the stirring views of both Lake Michigan, Crystal Lake and the landscape of the golf course, but playing the hole well demands nothing short of a player's full concentration.

311
YARDS
___
PAR 4

The tall native grasses squeeze both sides of the first fairway.

1926: Mackenzie and Maxwell are first invited to the site, and they are eventually paid $5,000 for the design work at Crystal Downs.

1991: Crystal Downs plays host to the U.S. Senior Amateur. The winner is Bill Bosshard who, at the tender age of 55 years 3 months and 18 days becomes the youngest champion in the history of the Senior Amateur.

1996: Golf Digest rates Crystal Downs 13th on the magazine's "100 Greatest" list, as well as the 2nd "Best in State" course for the years 1995 through 1998.

DEFINING
MOMENTS

1989: Despite being well-received by Golf Digest's course-rating panel for years, Crystal Downs doesn't appear on the magazine's "100 Greatest" list until this year.

Cypress Point Club

Location:	**Monterey, California**
Opened:	**1928**
Architect:	**Alister Mackenzie**
Par:	**72**
Length:	**6,536 yards**

The delicate 15th is a fitting prelude to the grandeur of the 16th.

The Monterey Peninsula is famous golf land to be sure, perhaps even America's most famous, but in the litany of saintly golf properties that occupy this enchanting stretch of the California coastline, none evokes such Holy Grail-like awe as the Alister Mackenzie masterpiece of Cypress Point. Indeed, no less a figure than golf historian and past USGA president Sandy Tatum summed up the romantic attachment to Cypress Point when he called it "the Sistine Chapel of golf."

Weighty stuff, but Cypress Point can be as spectacular as any religious experience. Though it has become more hidden from the public eye now that it is not part of the rotation of courses used for the Pebble Beach National Pro-Am, its allure remains palpable. There are few sites in America, or anywhere else, that could match what Mackenzie was presented with at Cypress Point. Indeed, Mackenzie related as much in writing a report for the club prospectus, as detailed in Tom Doak's fine biography, *The Life and Works of Dr. Alister Mackenzie.* "I have no hesitation in saying that in the beauty of its surroundings, the magnificence of its sand dunes, its spectacular sea views, its glorious cypress trees there is an opportunity of making a course which should be superior to any other."

The result of Mackenzie's work is, as Herbert Warren Wind has written, "an almost incomparable variety of holes." Settings move in and around wild sand dunes, ocean cliffs, forests and back again in what Tom Watson called "a combination of beauty and difficulty." Despite a syncopated scorecard that includes four par 5s in the first 10 holes (two back-to-back), a stretch of four par 4s in a row, followed by consecutive par 3s, the rhythm of the golf course seems to build gently. Or hauntingly, according to the legendary Dave Marr, who once said, "All day you're twisting in the wind, waiting for the 16th to appear."

The par-3 16th is without question as majestic an experience as can be found in a single golf hole anywhere. Still, while it is the high note at Cypress Point, it is not the entire melody. Indeed, while you get a sense of the ocean from the very first tee and throughout the round, it does not appear as an integral part of a golf hole until the 15th, only slightly less dramatic an ocean-carry par 3 than the 16th. Nor is the 17th, the third straight ocean hole, to be overlooked, with its dogleg around a patch of gnarled trees back toward a green that appears closer to the cliffs than it actually is.

Elsewhere, though, the challenges are the same, with slightly less distracting backdrops. Working intimately with the lay of the land, Mackenzie offers an array of short par 4s and reachable par 5s that tantalize and torment. A prime example is the 292-yard ninth, which is set along a ridge of dunes. At once, the peril of an unsuccessful bold play with a driver or 3-wood is weighed against the challenge of hitting two precise iron shots, one to a snaking fairway, the second to a tiny green amidst an ocean of bunkers and dunes. And, of course, with the sea so close, there is always the wind to further complicate the issue.

Despite its demanding landscape and testing holes, Cypress Point remains a course that fully rewards excellent shotmaking. That was the case during an epic match played by Byron Nelson and Ben Hogan against aspiring amateurs Ken Venturi and Harvie Ward in which the foursome recorded 27 birdies and an eagle. Said Nelson later, "Cypress Point is one of the most inspiring places in the world to play this game, and it is the kind of course where, if you play really well, you can score."

1926: Marion Hollins shows designer Seth Raynor that the site for the 16th hole, which he thought to be too difficult as a par 3, is quite playable by teeing up a ball and driving it right across the inlet.

1990: Mark O'Meara wins the AT&T Pebble Beach National Pro-Am for the second consecutive year and the last time the tournament's rotation of courses includeds Cypress Point Club.

DEFINING MOMENTS

1956: Ben Hogan and Byron Nelson defeat amateurs Harvie Ward and Ken Venturi on the 18th green in a "friendly" match that features 67s by Ward and Nelson, a 65 from Venturi and a 63 by Hogan.

The snaking par–4 ninth is lined with tumult.

Feature Hole

16

It is almost insulting to attempt to describe the grandeur of Cypress Point's 16th hole within the normal lexicon of golfing terms. New words and perhaps a whole other language should be invented instead. A monstrous challenge disguised in splendor, the 16th stands alone among great one-shot holes—*Golf Digest* fittingly named it the best par-3 hole in American golf at the end of the 20th century. From the tee it looks at once impossible and irresistible. And yet it is not relentless. A shorter, safer route is available left of the green, leaving a nervy pitch-and-putt for par. While the best of professionals have recorded some unusual numbers here, including a 16 by Ed "Porky" Oliver, Bing Crosby reportedly once made an ace here. But that makes sense. A hole like this definitely has a sense of style.

231 YARDS

PAR 3

Desert Forest Golf Club

Location: **Carefree, Arizona**
Opened: **1962**
Architect: **Red Lawrence**
Par: **72**
Length: **7,035 yards**

These days, when the phrase "desert golf" is often tossed around, a pretty clear image comes to mind of an unforgiving golf course set in arid lands with saguaro and desert washes typically in play, where anything off the fairway is literally in the desert. It's common knowledge now. The reason it's common knowledge is because of what Red Lawrence achieved at Desert Forest Golf Club at the beginning of the 1960s.

Desert Forest is an American golf course design landmark. Working with the natural rolls in the desert landscape, Lawrence gracefully set out a demonically simple design, meticulously fitting holes in between the harsher elements. Indeed, Lawrence built no adjoining fairways and let the slopes move gently around the property, which changes some 400 feet from high point to low. He made room for just 55 acres or so of grass, and in so doing his course became the gold standard in the type of golf that would drive the Arizona tourism industry. From the very outset, Desert Forest was an acknowledged wonder, called by many the "Pine Valley of the West."

Weighty praise indeed, but when you consider that Desert Forest's layout includes not one single fairway bunker, although its slope rating is an astronomical 149, you realize that this layout demands the same sort of precision as the more famous, less barren layout in the East.

Architect Jay Morrish, whose designs in the desert with Tom Weiskopf, like Troon and the TPC of Scottsdale, have drawn great praise of their own, sees Desert Forest as both beauty and beast. "Desert Forest is a beautiful but difficult course," he says. "It's very fair, but very hard. It's one of Tom's favorites." Indeed, Weiskopf has bolstered the layout in recent years by adding some length to a few holes, but that has been the extent of the alterations. It is, as it always has been, an abruptly straightforward proposition, impecca-

At Desert Forest's 18th hole, the miss areas may be unforgiving but at least they are pretty.

bly maintained. The fairways are wide enough to accommodate the slight mishit, but without question one of Desert Forest's strengths is that it encourages a full examination with the most difficult club in the bag, the driver. On every side, the player is presented with what on one hand is the shimmering beauty of the desert landscape, and on the other its overwhelming hostility to poorly played golf shots.

The layout is target-style golf, yet nowhere does it seem overly contrived. There are forced carries over desert outcroppings, to be sure, but the real challenge is not to think about the imminent death of a miss to either the left or the right. And with the traditionally firm fairways, the misses do not have to be extraordinarily substantial. Starting with the first hole, nearly half the holes have some degree of bend to them, meaning a straight drive can often end up in trouble.

Some of the more memorable moments include the right-angle dogleg first, which lets you play your slice right out of the box; the bold diagonal carry over desert scrub on the dogleg-left, 453-yard fifth hole; the sweeping 393-yard 10th hole, which bends to the right, the same side where the troubling desert scrub lies in wait; the downhill 212-yard 17th, whose green seems almost overlooked amid the cholla and saguaro and encroaching badlands; and the meaty closer, which plays 464 straight-arrow yards.

Even though it is the founding father of desert golf, its challenge is decidedly current. Phil Mickelson, a multiple winner in the state as a Tour player and a long-time resident, appreciates its demands. "My favorite course in Arizona is Desert Forest. It's very simple, straightforward and natural. To me it is hands down the best course in the state."

Feature Hole

7

Named by esteemed golf writer Dan Jenkins as one of the best golf holes in America, the meaty seventh is the kind of desert golf, risk-reward par 5 that was invented by Red Lawrence at Desert Forest. From the tee, the player has two wildly different options to a split fairway. Fly it to the left for the safe three-shot route, or bust one 230 or more yards on the fly to the unseen target on the right, obscured by desert scrub and tall saguaro. The safe second is a layup short of the desert wash that slithers in front of the green, while the bold route on the right gives the player a direct line to the green, but again the wash must be carried. Typical of everywhere at Desert Forest, missing the fairway means you will, in all likelihood, be dodging cacti and rattlesnakes and the only thing you're likely to find will be a double bogey.

534 YARDS
PAR 5

The stifling par–3 17th reveals Lawrence as a master of the art of desert golf.

1960: Locating a substantial underground water basin, Arizonans Tom Darlington and K.T. Palmer establish the planned community of Carefree. They select Red Lawrence to do the golf course design.

1973: For the first time in its history, the Pacific Coast Amateur is held at a site other than on the West Coast. Mike Brannan (below) is the champion and the only player to finish the week under par.

DEFINING MOMENTS

1966: Just four years after opening, Desert Forest is listed in *Golf Digest*'s first-ever ranking of America's 100 Greatest Courses. It is the only Arizona course to appear on the list every year it has been published.

1990: Jackie Cummings became the youngest winner of the U.S. Senior Amateur, holing his only birdie of the day at the final hole to defeat Bobby Clark 3&2. The low score in the 36-hole qualifying rounds is six-over-par 150.

The 18th at East Lake is long, hard, unforgiving— and one shot.

East Lake Golf Club

Location: **Atlanta, Georgia**
Opened: **1908**
Architects: **Donald Ross (1915)/Rees Jones (1995)**
Par: **72**
Length: **7,196 yards**

Surely the home course of Bobby Jones merits some special rank among the most important clubs in the history of the game. But then that is mere historical affectation. Nearly a century after Jones first won the club championship as a young boy, the fully restored East Lake Golf Club still poses a supreme challenge for the best players the game can offer and stands as a thriving testament to Jones and the course he first played.

How solid is the layout at East Lake still? Well, when Hal Sutton rallied for a playoff victory at the 1998 Tour Championship, among his first words to the assembled media were, "Man, what a hard golf course this is. This week I think the golf course won."

Thanks in full measure to the careful hand of Rees Jones in reinvigorating the fading layout in the 1990s to a state beyond even its earlier glory, the reestablishment of East Lake is resounding on so many levels. The $100 million restoration included a massive investment in redeveloping the surrounding rundown community, and Jones' work on the course was crucial to the success of the overall project.

Interestingly, but not surprisingly, Donald Ross' routing was relatively unchanged by Jones some 80 years after Ross had totally reworked the original Tom Bendelow design. David Duval, who as a student at Georgia Tech played the declining East Lake layout prior to Jones' revival, knew it was of championship caliber even if it wasn't in championship condition. "Even when it was in bad shape, the layout itself was as good as I saw anywhere in the country," he remembers. "The place is unbelievable. The place is pure."

Ross was a master at plotting the rhythm of 18 holes, and the flow of the round at East Lake, through subtle but impressive elevation change and around the 27-acre lake, makes for a consummate challenge. There are water hazards in play, but none is unfair. In fact, only once is water a particularly dominant feature, fittingly at the shortest hole on the course. There is movement in the landscape, but it is always measured to the hole's strategy. And while the overwhelming theme is demanding par 4s, the championship layout affords the bigger hitters the chance to reach both of the par 5s in two shots.

There is a wonderful pace between the long and the short holes at East Lake. On the front nine, the player requires an equal mix of power and finesse for the tee shots. Four times the landing area is guarded by bunkers, three times it isn't, and the first half of the day includes the nervy island par 3 and a rollicking par 5 that tumbles downhill toward the lake and a heavily bunkered green tugging on the player's aggressive nature.

On the back nine, the challenge builds as does the scenery of the lake and the Atlanta skyline in the distance, visible from the 16th tee. The closing stretch is noteworthy from the 15th hole on. Players face an eminently reachable par 5, back-to-back stout par 4s (including the long 17th with East Lake at the left and a classically rolling green) and conclude the round with one of the all-time great finishing holes in golf. A full 232 yards uphill to a bi-level green, it is sure evidence that you have to earn your way into East Lake's historic museum of a clubhouse. Joked Duval about the brutal one-shotter, "Every course should have a driveable par 4."

Once again, East Lake is a thrilling test from beginning to end. As Tom Cousins, the developer who saved the course and East Lake's surrounding community, puts it, "Those are Bobby Jones' spike marks in the floor. When you're out here, you feel like you're walking on hallowed ground."

1915: Bobby Jones, who previously had won the club's children's and junior tournaments, wins the club championship at age 13, defeating his father in the final.

1963: Changes to the course were made in an effort to elevate its challenge for the 15th Ryder Cup matches. Bobby Jones calls the new course "beautiful," and the Americans win in a rout, 23–9.

1998: Completing a miraculous resurrection of his career, Hal Sutton wins the Tour Championship by defeating Vijay Singh in a sudden-death playoff. Sutton birdies the 18th to claim his richest prize in golf to date.

DEFINING
MOMENTS

1994: As part of a major refurbishment of the club, Rees Jones restores and refortifies the original Ross layout. Within three years, it is named one of America's 100 Greatest Courses, ending a 30-year absence.

2001: Bubba Dickerson wins the U.S. Amateur, defeating Robert Hamilton one-up in the final after rallying from a five-down deficit.

Despite the bunkers the best angle off the tee at the 13th is up the left center of the fairway.

Feature Hole

6

East Lake is home to a marvellous collection of short holes, especially the nifty downhill second with its benched green and the leviathan-sized closer, which plays close to 240 yards uphill and often into the wind. But its most photogenic and most unnerving hole might be the sixth, among the very first island greens ever designed in American golf. Tucked on an edge of the oversized East Lake, the smallish green appears microscopic, lost in the background of water. The only bailout is a bunker short and left, but recovery shots are no guarantee at the frighteningly sloped green. Increasing the anxiety is a prevailing wind that pushes the ball to the right and the lake. According to local lore, Bobby Jones was often stymied by this particular par 3: "What did you use on this hole?" Jimmy Demaret once asked Jones. "A water ball," Jones deadpanned.

164 YARDS

PAR 3

Firestone Country Club (South)

Location: **Akron, Ohio**
Opened: **1928**
Architect: **W.H. Way/Robert Trent Jones (1958)**
Par: **70**
Length: **7,139 yards**

Designed originally as a pleasant little perk for company employees, the South Course at Firestone Country Club eventually became one of the game's more complete examinations of skill and fortitude. Of course, only one man could effect such dramatic and lasting change, modern golf architecture's relentlessly vigilant visionary, Robert Trent Jones.

Jones was brought to Firestone in 1958 to orchestrate a redesign that would bring the South Course up to speed as a legitimate test for the 1960 PGA Championship. In his own special fashion, Jones, put the South Course on architectural steroids. He added 600 yards in length, fashioned two greenside ponds, integrated more than 50 new bunkers, and reinvigorated the greens with slopes and swerves. Then, just to show he meant business, he reduced par from 72 to 70.

Jones did not obliterate the original 1929 layout designed by English émigré Bertie Way, runner-up in the 1899 U.S. Open. In fact, the routing of largely parallel fairways remains much as it always did. Jones just stretched it out and toughened it up, turning diversion into hard labor.

Even in all its glory, Firestone is not overtly winsome. From above, at least half the holes appear stacked on top of each other like strips of bacon. Seven of the 12 par 4s play to at least 440 yards, five of those on the front side. There is no whimsy to the proceedings, no driveable par 4s, and three of the par 3s play at least 200 yards. It is a big hitters' special, and its list of winners generally bears this out. Jack Nicklaus and Tiger Woods have combined for eight victories here, including three in a row by Woods. Among Woods' stretch was a dominant performance in the gloaming in 2000, where a closing birdie left him 11 clear of the field thanks to a record-setting 259 total.

There is, of course, a certain sameness to the rhythm at Firestone that can make a round here a test of attrition. It led

There are no tricks at Firestone, particularly at the straightarrow finishing hole.

Nicklaus to suggest once that Firestone can even be a little boring. "You can fall asleep on it because you're always hitting the same kind of shots—woods or long irons," he said. While technology has left the longer players hitting some short irons into a few of those monstrous par 4s, the marching orders for the slog at Firestone remain the same: drive it long and drive it straight, or risk getting stuck behind one of the many trees that line every fairway. Firestone is not routinely pinched by bunkers in the landing areas. Nevertheless, many of the fairway bunkers are deep enough to alter the preferred route. Jones also managed to complete his refortification without the extensive use of water hazards, although the two he did install that front the third and 16th holes can be especially troubling. Just ask Arnold Palmer, who made a triple-bogey eight at the 16th

hole in throwing away his chances at the 1960 PGA Championship.

Although the course's yardage seems stout for a par 70, the rolling terrain can soften some of the longer par 4s like the third, ninth and 18th. But the greens are always guarded, often by the kind of bunkers that resist recovery. Even on the 12th, the shortest hole on the course, a benign par 3 becomes a menace thanks to a tabletop green and three deep bunkers that add salt to the wound of any misplayed shot.

But that may be the only appearance that is deceiving at Firestone. For the most part, it is about as hard to figure out as a bridge abutment—and just as yielding. "Firestone is one of the most straightforward courses you can play," Nicklaus says. "Everything is right there in front of you." And that would be the difference between boring, and just plain hard.

Feature Hole

16

One of two holes where Robert Trent Jones added a water hazard during his renovation prior to the 1960 PGA Championship, the 16th is an extra-large par 5 where both the lay up second shot and the approach shot are dicey propositions. To position the ball ideally for the third shot, the downhill second shot must find its way down to a large flat area without going too far into the pond cutting in on the right. Today, some of the bolder younger players have a go at this green in two, but not without a measure of fear. The hole typifies the term "signature hole," a phrase Jones himself invented. Arnold Palmer, who made an eight there to end his chances at the 1960 PGA Championship, simply called it "The Monster." He later wrote of the 16th; "It is a hole that is wisely played for par and dangerous to play for a birdie."

625 YARDS

PAR 5

The first hole sets the tone at Firestone—and it never veers far from it.

1960: Jay Hebert wins the PGA Championship at the redesigned Firestone with a one-over-par four-round total of 281, the only time the winner of the PGA finished with an over-par total.

1990: Jose Maria Olazabal sets a course record with a 61 in the first round and goes on to win the NEC World Series of Golf by a tour record 12 shots.

DEFINING MOMENTS

1975: Jack Nicklaus makes a miraculous scrambling five on the 16th hole in the third round, including a tee shot into the water and a 30-foot par putt, and goes on to win the PGA Championship for the fifth time.

2001: Tiger Woods wins for the third time in a row at Firestone, defeating Jim Furyk in a seven-hole playoff at the World Golf Championship's NEC Invitational.

The still East Harbor belies the name given to the 13th hole: Waterloo.

Fishers Island Club

Location: **Fishers Island, New York**
Opened: **1926**
Architect: **Seth Raynor**
Par: **72**
Length: **6,566 yards**

Seth Raynor did not train to be a golf course architect, never once saw the great linksland of the game's birth in Scotland and never really took to golf as his personal choice of recreation. The above seems laughably impossible, given what Raynor did at Fishers Island Club, a majestic reflection of the beauty of the game placed in as invigorating a setting as there is in all of golf. Few places exude the very soul of the game at its best as does Fishers Island. Despite having just a passing interest in actually playing the game, Raynor knew what characterized great golf and great settings. He combined both effortlessly and brilliantly in one of the few true American linksland courses.

Ultra-exclusive to the point of nearly being invisible, Fishers Island is not on the way to anywhere. Although it belongs to New York, the island is best accessed from a ferry leaving New London on the Connecticut coast. What awaits the few who are welcomed is what some have called the Cypress Point of the East. (There's a measure of hyperbole in that sentiment, and a bit of truth, as well. Indeed, Raynor was supposed to be the architect at Cypress Point before his untimely death of pneumonia in 1926 at age 51.) What Raynor did at Fishers Island was nothing short of golf magic. Every tee and every green of every hole has a view of the ocean, with some holes looking out across the sound to Connecticut in the distance.

Raynor was C.B. Macdonald's on-site right-hand man, directing, modifying and enhancing Macdonald's plans at courses like Chicago Golf Club, Lido and Piping Rock. Raynor saw what Macdonald wanted to do with great conceptual design of holes like the Redan, Punchbowl, Biarritz, Cape and Eden, and put it into practical terms that fit the topography they were walking on for a particular course.

At Fishers Island, Raynor carried over that same theme of paying homage to the great design concepts, but his careful hand presented each of the old favorites in a way so new as to make their challenge permanent and unfading. Indeed, as adept as Macdonald was at this art of imitation, his student Raynor's work at Fishers Island, at least given the setting, was everybit the equal of the master, perhaps even superior.

The examples are plenty at Fishers Island, extraordinarily so with the par 3s. The Redan second hole stands exposed to the constant breeze and less-than-well-struck shots can be punished by a pond in front. The Biarritz fifth is a majestically original adaptation, playing as much as 229 yards to a green on a ledge surrounded by deep gouges of sand, and, as with so many holes, the flag stands silhouetted against an unending expanse of ocean water. The Eden 11th hole is yet another exquisite par 3, Long Island Sound seemingly enveloping the green and the golfer's self-confidence. The

14th is a full-throated par 4 in the style of the Cape hole, where the golfer with designs on greatness cannot play safe and expect to score well. Fisher Island's eighth is a variation on the theme of the Old Course's Road hole, but instead of a blind shot over a hotel, the shot here is over a section of beach, just as intimidating, but a much better view.

If Macdonald ushered in the idea of heroic architecture, Raynor enhanced that belief at Fishers Island, but added a measure of the poetic. If golf course architects are ever said to have a muse, then Raynor clearly exhibited such fervor in his plan at Fishers Island. He did not live to see it completed, but should he somehow be transported to the layout today, he would recognize it immediately. Like the great treasure that it is, Fishers Island Club has been preserved, its challenge just as real, its beauty just as inspiring as ever.

1614: Fishers Island is discovered by European setter Adrian Block, for whom Block Island is named. The name may have come from one of Block's navigators, whose name was Vischers.

1969: Fishers Island Club makes its first appearance on *Golf Digest*'s ranking of America's 100 Greatest Courses, debuting in the "sixth ten" on the list.

DEFINING MOMENTS

1926: A residential park plan for Fishers Island is drawn up and the land comes under the control of the Fishers Island Development Corporation and includes the Fishers Island Club, as designed by Seth Raynor.

2001: Fishers Island is once again named to the list of America's 100 Greatest Courses. It is named No. 44 on the list, right behind Chicago Golf Club, Raynor's great collaborative effort with C.B. Macdonald.

The ample green at the short 16th is not without a measure of treachery.

Feature Hole

4

In earlier designs the two had collaborated on, Raynor and Macdonald had combined an Alps hole (originally made famous at Prestwick) with a Punchbowl green, where the green seems to be set in a valley. But Raynor elevates the concept to high art at Fishers Island, where the fourth hole is memorable in a course full of unforgettable moments. The green makes for the only blind second shot on the course, but the discomfort is tempered by the mammoth size of the putting surface, a mere 12,000 square feet. More than two-thirds of the green lies perched above the beach and ocean, a lingering reminder to the player that a bold play to this green can be costly. Despite there not being a single bunker from tee through green here, it still stands rated as the No. 1 handicap hole on the course.

397 YARDS

PAR 4

Garden City Golf Club

Location: **Garden City, New York**
Opened: **1899**
Architect: **Devereux Emmet/Walter Travis**
Par: **73**
Length: **6,911 yards**

The par–3 2nd hole's menace starts with a gaping pit and finishes with coffin-like bunkers.

Garden City Golf Club deliberately, steadfastly, happily remains a throwback. Here, for instance, jackets are required, even for breakfast. Of course, the most shining example of its status as a living, breathing anachronism lies in its simple, mercurial, invigorating golf course. In so many ways, its design would never be attempted today. Indeed, the tendency would be to try to do so much more to the landscape to create a golf course, instead of merely uncovering one. Yet Garden City Golf Club's ancient design, so uncomplicated and overtly natural, continues to be even more inspiring and more wildly full of life than most golf courses a tenth its age.

The object early on at Garden City Golf Club was to construct a links on land perfectly suitable and perfectly reminiscent of Scotland. The sandy soil of Long Island's Hempstead Plain, just minutes from Manhattan, produced naturally firm turf, while typical wind conditions gave the whole place an ideal golf feel. Never mind that the sea was a good 10 miles away, here was pure golf turf. Both original architect Devereux Emmet and later Walter Travis, the "Grand Old Man" of early American golf and the patron saint of Garden City Golf Club, simply sought to uncover it. In fact, Emmet hardly moved any turf and kept most of the natural contours he found in the fairways. Travis merely made it harder, revealing his belief that "a really good course must abound in hazards."

Garden City is a thrill ride for the golfing mind from the moment the round begins just steps outside the golf shop door until the instant the day ends just steps short of that same door. It is a series of challenging angles, insidious bunkering, brilliant contrasts (in both topography and colors), awkward mounds, endless variety and fulfilment. It achieves completely Travis' objective for the course, namely, "to compel a player to extract the full value from each and

every club in his bag during the round, and on one or two of the holes to play certain testing shots with such nicety and keen judgment as to make even the best player pause before attempting their execution."

That sort of judgment may be required more often than not at Garden City, but it comes with such a casual but effective sense of style and rhythm. The holes here are compelling in different ways. There are, for instance, four par 4s of 360 yards or less, where the golfer has to think he may do something productive, but they are counterbalanced by seven others of more than 400 yards where prudence should rule. Each of the par 5s requires a solid drive and then deep contemplation, for even the layup shots go beyond mere formality. The short holes can be heroic stuff, like the old quarry pit guarding the second and the rare par-3 finisher

over water. And always there are Garden City's pricklish bunkers. It is not unusual to see steps entering a greenside sand pit, nor is it strange to find your shot blocked by the steep face of a fairway bunker, like at the epic 440-yard sixth.

The greens are not bodacious affairs at Garden City, but more often than not they naturally flow out of the fairways, and from the proper angle will accept a run-up shot. But there is subtle deception here, too, says Emmet. "There is nothing to guide you as to distance as you would be guided by hills and exposed visible bunkers around the green."

Garden City is always about intense reflection and precise action. That is its joy. What Walter Travis once said about the game of golf rings just as true about Garden City Golf Club. Golf "cultivates patience and endurance under adversity," Travis explained, "and yet keeps alive the fires of hope."

Feature Hole

15

Tom Doak, the noted architect and design consultant to Garden City Golf Club from 1986–2001, singles out the 15th hole as the best at the club. On the scorecard it already rates as the most difficult. Says Doak in the club's official history, "While I don't believe there is a poor or uninteresting hole on the golf course, neither are there many which I would hold up as a contender for the best in the world, with the possible exception of the par-4 15th." No. 15 plays at nearly 450 yards with a 10-foot deep, trench-like cross bunker running the entire width of the fairway about 300 yards from the tee. Not a single bunker protects the green, but there's no need because it is strong enough to defend itself. It slopes severely from left to right, making putts right of the hole quite difficult.

447 YARDS

PAR 4

The 16th's smallish green is dwarfed by trouble in all directions.

1908: Jerry Travers defeats Walter Travis in the semi-final of the U.S. Amateur. Travis loses the final hole when his tee shot on the closing par 3 lands in a nasty bunker he himself had installed. It was later named in his honor.

1913: Jerry Travers wins a U.S. Amateur at Garden City for the second time in five years, not once winning a match by less than 3&2.

1914: Walter Travis wins the Spring Invitation tournament for the eighth time, including a stretch from 1902–10 when he won seven straight times. Following Travis's death in 1927, the event was renamed the Travis Memorial.

1924: In a contest much closer than the 9–3 margin indicated, the U.S. wins the Walker Cup over Great Britain and Ireland. Bobby Jones lost his four-ball match, his only loss ever in international team competition.

DEFINING **MOMENTS**

1974: George Burns III playing in an exhibition to celebrate the club's 75th anniversary makes ten birdies on his way to a 63 and a new course record.

Harbour Town Golf Links

Location: **Hilton Head Island, South Carolina**
Opened: **1969**
Architects: **Pete Dye and Jack Nicklaus**
Par: **71**
Length: **6,973 yards**

T he story goes that Pete Dye originally wasn't supposed to be involved in the design of the golf course that would come to be Harbour Town Golf Links. Good thing he got involved. Harbour Town may have been blessed with a soulfully scenic setting, but it was Dye's passion and creativity that transformed it from just another pretty face to an exhaustive mental examination. "With Harbour Town, we entered a new era in golf course architecture," said Rees Jones. "It raised the bar for the rest of us. It made us all better."

The Dye–Jack Nicklaus collaboration produced a demanding design founded on the idea of thinking more than hitting. To be sure, it could flex its muscle selectively, but Harbour Town is restrained on all sides by overhanging trees, bunkered devilishly in all the wrong places and finished with miniature greens that elicit the measured response, like a jeweler working with uncut diamonds. You do not subdue this golf course, you woo it, entreat it, almost caress it. And then hope the breeze doesn't become a gale.

Holes move at uncommon angles, greens seem uncomfortably positioned (almost invisibly set at the level of the surrounding fairways on occasion, too), so that a player must often think of even his preferred first putt before deciding on the line for his tee shot. Never one to settle for the way things were being done, Dye installed bunkers of shapes rarely seen in the architecture of the day. Gone were the prototypical matching oval pairs in the fairway landing areas, replaced by snakelike waste areas that could stretch along the edge of a fairway or green for as much as 90 yards, or others encircling a green like an unkempt moat. Trees found their way into the middle of fairways. Greens, occasionally were heart-shaped, the kind of targets that seemingly required reading glasses to see, all of them averaging between 2,000 and 3,500 square feet, less than half the going standard.

On the exposed 17th, the wind can wreak havoc with the mind and the golf ball.

Harbour Town demands precision, obviously, given that every hole has elements of trees, water and sand punishing anything that strays off the one true path. But the dangers are contained. Aside from the par 3s, there is not one hole that demands a forced carry, though occasionally the preferred line includes a direct shot over a wildly huge expanse of sand or marsh, like at the angular par-4 16th or, of course, the epic finishing hole. Overhanging branches enhance the trepidation on holes like No. 1, as well as the longish 11th, but frankly the surrounding jungle on almost every hole makes everything on this course seem a little tighter than it really is. Dye and Harbour Town play tricks with your head. The feel is clearly of a short course, but there are still four par 4s that stretch longer than 435 yards, and even the medium-length par 4s like the 12th play longer thanks to subtly infuriating doglegs.

On a course where precision is everything, it comes as little surprise that the par 3s are the crown jewels. Lagoons angle into each of the par 3s, and huge bunkers surround or abut the greens, but none are more dastardly than the 185-yard 17th, which often plays into the breeze to a green that from the tee looks no bigger than a dinner plate.

Harbour Town manages to intimidate quietly, it bends the golfer to its will without force-feeding him a steady diet of heroically penal design. Even with a recent upgrade, completely supervised by Dye, the course remains what it always has been. Says 1988 MCI Heritage winner Greg Norman, "You still have to keep fitting your shots to the hole. It still requires tactical position golf. That's why it remains one of the great golf courses of the world."

1969: Harbour Town's reputation gets a tremendous boost when Arnold Palmer wins the first-ever Heritage Classic at the brand new course, his first win in 14 months, with a birdie on the final hole.

1994: Hale Irwin becomes the tournament's oldest winner, defeating Greg Norman by two shots at the age of 48 years, ten months.

DEFINING
MOMENTS

1988: Greg Norman, playing in front of Jamie Hutton, a young cancer victim who had requested the chance to watch his hero play in a tournament, wins the MCI Heritage Classic by one shot, rallying with a final-round 66.

1998: Davis Love III cruises to a tournament-record seven-shot victory in winning at Harbour Town for a record fourth time. "Sorry I didn't give you much of a show," Love says after the commanding performance.

The bunker guarding the 13th hole is nearly the size of the green it defends.

Feature Hole

Harbour Town by nature is a course of confinement, so it can be a shock to the system to step out into the clearing of the 18th tee and see the wide open expanse of Calibogue Sound and the sheer enormity of the final hole. From the back tee, it is better than a 250-yard carry to reach the fairway on the ideal line. Completing the heroic path requires another long carry to the green, anything less than perfect winds up in trouble. Dye provides a safer line up the right side, but players must contend with out of bounds and trees, and of course a longer, riskier route to the green. The final fairway paints a dramatic picture as players work their way home to Harbour Town's trademark striped lighthouse. Dye and Nicklaus insisted on finishing the round with the 18th's majestic setting rather than manufacturing a hole that played its way back to the clubhouse. Certainly, after playing as fine a hole as the 18th, you can wait a while to change your shoes.

452 YARDS

PAR 4

Inverness Club

Location: **Toledo, Ohio**
Opened: **1919**
Architect: **Donald Ross**
Par: **71**
Length: **7,255 yards**

Some may quibble as to the Inverness Club's worthiness as a great golf design. They will point to the eight parallel fairways, the elimination of four original Donald Ross holes in favor of four "modern" holes in the late 1970s, the convolution of the course's basic Ross qualities caused by the contributions of assorted consulting architects. Even golf historian Herbert Warren Wind once suggested, "I gather that while Inverness proved to be a fairly testing layout [for the 1920 U.S. Open], spread over nice rolling terrain, it struck no one as a truly great course…Certainly it was not at all in the same class as Ross' masterpieces Seminole and Pinehurst No. 2."

And to an extent all of that is true. Inverness never gives one a sense of pyrotechnics. Nor does its setting overly enhance the drama of its holes. And over the years the changes to the course and the mix of renovating architects seem to be at least as much business decisions as artistic enhancements.

Like its predominant architect Donald Ross, though, Inverness is practical, functional, efficient golf, and its challenge lies squarely in its unyielding demand for precision in both thought and action. Inverness is very much straight line, point-to-point golf. The route here is always A to B to C; skipping a middle step often results in more regret than success. That is not to say that the route is unobstructed; there are 110 bunkers on the property, reflecting very much the philosophy of Ross on sand, which he once stated this way: "A golf course without bunkers is a very monotonous affair…Bunkers should be so placed as to be clearly in view, and in such locations as to make all classes of players think."

That they are at Inverness, directing traffic and forcing decisions. This is particularly so at the sporty collection of short par 4s, like the first, the 10th and especially the 18th. It is well worth noting that, despite the changes to the

The 17th hole is big and mean— like the bunker guarding the left side of the green.

course, the final 10 holes are exclusively Ross' handiwork, not significantly changed since he laid them out just after World War I. Typically, the balance is sheer perfection: three short par 4s, three medium-length par 4s, two long par 4s, a par 3 and a par 5. Half the holes make one believe that a birdie is possible, while the other half make sure you are fully stocked in the courage and patience department.

Though some of Ross' original work has been lost to the demands of technology and talent (the old seventh hole, a short par 4 with a menacing chasm in play, was a loss mourned by many), the new holes beef up the challenge enough for Inverness to remain a championship test. Dick Wilson refortified the layout in 1956, while George Fazio built four new holes at Inverness in preparation for the 1979 U.S. Open. Ironically, the highlight of the changes might be the new seventh hole, a 481-yard behemoth with a nasty, snaking stream along the right side and a gently elevated green with a wicked slope from back to front. Yet for all its difficulty, there is not a single bunker from tee to green.

In a way, the challenge at Inverness has a way of wearing on a player over the course of a tournament. In its major championships, Inverness has been remembered as often for its loser, the man who stumbled down the stretch. Harry Vardon, Cary Middlecoff and Greg Norman all had unfortunate ends at Inverness, as much because the course allowed others to rally as it was able to exact a toll on the leader.

It is a simple but ideal test, says Byron Nelson. "Inverness may lack the aesthetic charm of a Pebble Beach or a Cherry Hills," he once said, "but it is a solid, honest course that demands precise and accurate shotmaking."

Feature Hole

18

Lost in this modern age of 350-yard drives is the simple torture reserved for the short par 4. Few were better at it than Donald Ross, who once wrote in *Golf Has Never Failed Me*, "In holes of this length, both the drive and approach should be difficult." Not generally driveable, the 18th hole at Inverness is golf at its finest, a test of will and guile and finesse, not brute strength. Here, a bold player could take a driver in hopes of getting up by the green, but a more prudent play is a fairway wood or long iron. Still, five bunkers on both sides of the slim fairway protect the landing area, asking the player to consider laying back but leaving himself a longer club in. Another three pits guard the front of the tiny green. Said Jack Nicklaus, "It is the hardest easy hole I've ever played."

354 YARDS

PAR 4

The creek makes the short 10th quaint and troublesome.

1920: Harry Vardon, leading by five strokes with seven holes to play, drops eight shots to par on his final seven holes to lose the U.S. Open to Ted Ray.

1931: Billy Burke and George Von Elm are tied at the end of regulation in the U.S. Open. A 36-hole playoff is held the next day, and again they finish tied. Burke finally prevails by a single stroke after the next day's 36 holes.

DEFINING MOMENTS

1979: In the U.S. Open, Lon Hinkle plays to the eighth fairway on the par-5 17th hole and reaches the green in two. By the next morning, a tree is installed, forever known as the "Hinkle Tree," blocking that route.

1986: In the PGA Championship Greg Norman stumbles with a final round 76, allowing Bob Tway to catch him and beat him on the 18th green, stunning the golf world by holing a bunker shot for a birdie.

Kiawah Island (Ocean Course)

Location: **Kiawah Island, South Carolina**	
Opened: **1991**	
Architect: **Pete Dye**	
Par: **72**	
Length: **7,296 yards**	

Dye wasn't sure the 17th was dramatic enough, so he added a lake; mission accomplished.

Kiawah's Ocean Course truly is a thing of epic beauty. From every hole, the Atlantic Ocean is in view, soothing in its vastness. While there are no forests in its landscape, the scraggly oaks that dot the Ocean Course's edges, all seemingly pruned by the constant wind, provide an almost artistic contrast to the setting. Sea oats and tall native grasses accent the surroundings, as much a part of the grand stage as the wide stretches of sand and marshland that frame every hole. How something so stirring can at once be so ghastly merciless would seem improbable were it not for the frenetically insidious gifts of one devilish golf genius. Only Pete Dye could find a way to bring golf and nature together to inspire such conflicting (but closely related) emotions. Even at its fiercest, the Ocean Course exudes the paradigm for every golf course: it inspires in the golfer as much wonder as it does fear, from first tee to 18th green.

Dye knew the layout could be special, especially since he was given more than two-and-a-half miles of uninterrupted coastline to work with. It's a course of masterful angles and daring physical challenge that wear on a golfer's insides. Even as holes parallel the ocean and run for stretches in the same general direction, the preferred line seems to change constantly. Sand dunes eat into the right side of the seventh hole, but encroach on the left at the ninth hole, so the proper attack is altered though the two holes play in the same direction. It is a series of adjustments to navigate the Ocean Course, a series of risks to be taken, or not.

As the series of golf catastrophes played out in the 1991 Ryder Cup attest, the Ocean Course can be brutish. Indeed, Dye had installed additional sets of tees so the course could play as long as 7,800 yards if necessary. (For struggling golfers, it can seem at least that long regardless of its actual length.) But while it can be exceptionally nasty, it does not play like a behemoth. For instance, never at the Ocean

Course is there a long forced carry for a shot from the fairway. Rather, from the tee, the carries are more a game of the possible, rather than an edict of the mandatory. Dye's real genius lies in how he makes the golfer want to challenge his angles. The carry over a deep waste area or marsh or pond always seems eminently doable, but because the target is angled to the line of play, a slight miss can put the ball in a hazard, or leave a longer second shot than is ideal.

A perfect example might be the 439-yard 10th hole, where the more a player challenges the water to the right, the more open his line becomes to the well-guarded green. Especially impressive, too, are the inventive par 3s, like the redan-like 14th and the vicious, watery 17th, a hole that caused calamity for Mark Calcavecchia at the 1991 Ryder Cup, where he deposited two balls in the pond. Like the course itself, the hole is raw and uncompromising, where even safe shots can lead to frustration.

Still, Dye makes the overall design work in any degree of the omnipresent wind. The fairways are wide to accommodate all sorts of optional play from the tee, and many of the longer holes have greens that offer a ground route as well as one through the air. The greens themselves are each unique works of art, with swoops and swales and plateaus that while manmade seem perfectly natural to their setting.

In the fullest of terms, Kiawah's Ocean Course is the supreme test on a site of unsurpassed beauty. "There's not another course remotely like it," Dye said at its unveiling. "My only goal was to provide a course resort guests enjoy enough to want to come back." They will, provided they exchange their scorecards for postcards.

1989: Despite there being no actual course in existence, the PGA of America names Kiawah Island to be the site for the 1991 Ryder Cup matches. The course would originally be known as the Sam Ryder Course.

1991: On the final missed putt of the final match of the final day, the Americans claim victory over Europe in the Ryder Cup, 14½-13½, the first U.S. win since 1983.

1997: The Ocean Course is host to the team World Cup of Golf and Ireland's Padraig Harrington and Paul McGinley claim the team title and Scotland's Colin Montgomerie wins the individual title.

DEFINING **MOMENTS**

2001: In a return to the scene of the crime for many European and American stars, an over-40 team competition is held at the Ocean Course. The Americans come from behind to defeat the International squad 12½-11½.

Feature Hole

2

When you step to the tee on the second hole, you immediately realize you're in a whole different universe. With a tee box that stares into the Atlantic and a fairway that bounds like the sea, the occasionally reachable par 5 asks the best players to fire a bullet draw off the tee and then somehow feather a long iron or fairway wood to a shelf of a green with a sometimes hidden flag. Guarding the miss areas left and right are marsh and waste bunkers and seemingly acres of wild sea oats and wire grasses. The tempered route is not without its fear factor either, as a rivulet of marsh cuts through the fairway about 130 yards from the green, which sits between sand dunes front and back. How difficult can this hole play? During the singles matches of the 1991 Ryder Cup, Seve Ballesteros won the second with a seven to Wayne Levi's eight.

528 YARDS

PAR 5

Every nook and cranny of the 9th hole seems home to despair.

84

Los Angeles Country Club (North)

Location: **Los Angeles, California**
Opened: **1921**
Architect: **George C. Thomas Jr.**
Par: **71**
Length: **6,909 yards**

George Thomas, who never accepted a fee for his golf design work and was even better at growing roses than he was at building golf courses, was not much of a softie when it came to the playing of the game. In his mind, golf was a game played as much with the challenge of the land as with the challenge of the swing. In his definitive book on golf design, *Golf Architecture in America*, he writes, "Let there be nothing between the tee and the green but perfect fairway, and the green itself absolutely level, and what would be the result? A thing without interest or beauty, on which there is no thrill of accomplishment."

Knowing this, it is easy to understand the motivation behind his wonderfully rolling design at the North Course at The Los Angeles Country Club, which is clearly a thing of equally substantial measures of both interest and beauty. Surrounded by views of the distant skyscrapers of downtown Los Angeles, LACC is an oasis of ridges, hollows and sweeping terrain, accented expertly with golf holes that not only fit their immediate landscape but test the golfer's full arsenal in 18 distinct ways.

At LACC North, Thomas took an original routing by Herbert Fowler, and with the help of his right-hand man, William Bell, he redirected it as his own. The course plays decidedly downhill on occasion, but there are plenty of approach shots to elevated greens and an array of interesting angles and stances—the kind that ideally inspire certainty of both plan and action.

Though Thomas starts the day with consecutive par 5s, he balances the challenge of the first nine with a couple of shorter par 4s, including an immediate change of pace at the tactical 386-yard third hole with its frenetically bouncy fair-

The claustrophobic 6th somehow gets harder the safer you play it.

way and beastly front bunker. Even more nifty is the fish-hook-shaped, 355-yard sixth. With the tee nearly 100 feet above the fairway, bold players in years past were tempted to drive the green over a narrow barranca. Although the lengthening of the hole and the growth of trees has made that less tempting than in the original design, the narrow green makes even a wedge approach as delicate as needlepoint.

Don't be surprised by the quintet of par-3 holes at LACC North, either. Thomas indicated in his writings that such a setup provided more intensity for the typical player. Here, they are a generally stern lot, highlighted, of course, by the epic 11th. Still, holes like the 233-yard seventh and the sporty, 132-yard 15th demonstrate Thomas' mastery of the entire one-shot hole spectrum.

Today, the best examples of Thomas' work can be found on the back nine, in particular the 16th. The crowned fairway set along a ridge makes precision with a driver exceptionally valuable. A bunker and steep drop encourage safe play up the right side, but truthfully the bold line up the left side provides a better angle to a green that slopes, not gently, from left to right. The 16th features one of Thomas' deceptive bunkers, a high-lipped trap placed well short of the putting surface.

With Thomas, even the deceptions look natural. As he writes in *Golf Architecture in America*, "In golf construction, art and utilty meet; both are absolutely vital; one is utterly ruined without the other…The contours of our tees, of our hazards, of our rough and of our fairways should, except when otherwise absolutely necessary, all melt into the land surrounding them." At LACC, in Thomas' hands, they all do.

Feature Hole

George Thomas suggested that, given the right topography, he'd accept a 300-yard par 3. The 11th doesn't quite measure that long, but it proves his point. A long downhill shot to a murderously bunkered green set on a plateau and sloping from left to right illustrates Thomas' passion for the difficult one-shotter. You cannot be indifferent and get away with it on this hole, which is occasionally referred to as a "reverse Redan," where the hole is attacked with a left-to-right shot to match the slope in the green. Thomas neatly provides a bail-out area left of the green that actually allows the smartly played ball to bounce onto the putting surface. From the tee, the distant skyline of downtown Los Angeles shimmers through the smog, providing as much a pleasing respite from the preceding rigors of play as a distraction to the immediate task at hand.

245 YARDS

PAR 3

The 9th green is enveloped by the trademark bunkering of Thomas and Bell.

1897: A number of Los Angeles men build a makeshift course on an old garbage dump. The holes are fashioned by burying nine tomato cans in the ground. Within a year, the club has more than 100 members.

1926: Harry Cooper, who garners the nickname "Lighthorse" for his speedy and dominant play during the week, wins the first-ever L.A. Open with a score of five-under 279, three shots better than George Von Elm.

1930: Glenna Collett Vare (below) defeats Virginia Van Wie 6&5 in the U.S. Women's Amateur final, her third in a row and fifth of six overall titles. It is the first U.S. Women's Amateur played west of Missouri.

1934: Macdonald Smith wins the Los Angeles Open for the fourth and final time in a six-year span. His 280 total is eight shots better than runners-up Bill Melhorn and Willie Hunter.

DEFINING
MOMENTS

1940: Lawson Little wins the L.A. Open, defeating Clayton Heafner by one shot with a four-day total of two-under-par 282. It will be the last time the L.A. tour event is played at Los Angeles Country Club.

At the 9th and so many other holes at Mauna Kea, the ocean looms, inspires and distracts.

Mauna Kea Golf Course

Location: **Kamuela, Hawaii**
Opened: **1965**
Architect: **Robert Trent Jones Sr.**
Par: **72**
Length: **7,165 yards**

It is hard to believe that Hawaii was not always a golf destination. With months of sunshine, ocean around every corner and gentle breezes that often turn into four-club howling gales, this is the environment that stirs the passion of any golfer. Of course, we know that now. One large reason Hawaii has become a golf paradise is that Robert Trent Jones Sr. showed it to us when he unveiled the legendary Mauna Kea, a garden of Eden of a golf course set amid a field of distractions that vary from unyielding black lava to the pounding surf of the Pacific Ocean.

But focusing on the stirring scenery at Mauna Kea misses its genius. First of all, it must be remembered that Jones broke new agronomic ground at Mauna Kea, constructing the course and growing grass on the remains of volcanic rock. It would illustrate the relentless pursuit Jones spoke of in his book, *Golf's Magnificent Challenge.* He writes, "On rare occasions, we are forced to tell a developer or clubbuilder that the land he has chosen is not suitable for a golf course. But I've really found very few places in my career where a golf course can't be built."

Not only did Jones manage to build a golf course on the stark fields of lava, he contrived a masterpiece. Here, Jones performed the sort of landscaping high-wire act that the best golf course architects make look easy. He naturally incorporates the awe-inspiring setting of Hawaii's Kohala Coast and the breathtaking views of both Mauna Kea Mountain and the monstrous active volcano Mauna Loa within the golf course. The course is not overwhelmed by its setting, but instead seems to move with it like the surf rolling into Kaunaoa Bay. Even though it is set along the shoreline, elevation on the golf course changes more than 300 feet, making for some wondrously bounding holes like the 394-yard second and the 247-yard, par-3 11th, which calls for a gently downhill shot to a green backed by what seems to be the entire Pacific Ocean. In fact, every hole at Mauna Kea provides views of one kind or another of the glistening ocean, none more inspiring than the storied third hole, the boomerang par 3 that plays more than 200 yards across a roiling inlet from one lava rock to a massive, rolling green set on another lava rock.

The holes move up and down the slopes against the sea here, and so at more than 7,000 yards and buffeted by a constant wind, Mauna Kea can be punishingly Jonesian on occasion—particularly at holes like the fourth with its uphill climb and vicious collection of five fairway bunkers, and the stretch of holes 12 through 17 where the yardages are full and the wind can wreak havoc. Particularly stout are the divided fairway 14th and the par-4 16th, where a stand of tall palms always seem to be in front of your approach shot.

Jones strives to test different levels in different ways, and one of the more definitive is how the widest landing areas (sometimes 50 and 60 yards wide to accommodate the healthy breezes) are those for the shorter hitters, while the areas that are most binding are the targets reserved for the better, longer-hitting players. While the course is free of water hazards (save the ocean on the third hole), just as he has done on the mainland, Jones requires tactics as well as execution here. The big blast isn't enough here, it must be precise, as well. This is the case on holes like the finisher, which has often been voted as one of Hawaii's toughest holes. The hole doglegs just enough to the right to hide the vista of the seascape below until you make the turn to the green. It's the kind of sight Jones surely knew would make the day seem worthwhile, regardless of your score.

1962: New York financier Laurance Rockefeller finds an idyllic, untouched piece of shoreline, and hires Robert Trent Jones Sr. to build a course that will be the centerpiece of a resort set on 1,800 ocean-side acres.

1965: A televised Big Three golf match is held at the brand-new course, pitting Arnold Palmer, Jack Nicklaus and Gary Player. Palmer and Nicklaus both shoot 31 on the back nine, which still stands as a course record.

1969: Mauna Kea debuts on *Golf Digest*'s ranking of America's 100 Greatest Courses. Mauna Kea was the highest-ranking Hawaiian course on the list that year and in six subsequent rankings.

DEFINING MOMENTS

1975: Several greens are softened to provide more enjoyment for the typical resort golfer that frequents Mauna Kea. Implementing the course changes is Jones' oldest son, Robert Trent Jones Jr.

Intimidated? Don't be. This is merely one of the third hole's forward tees.

Feature Hole

3

This hole is so majestic, that its back tee has spent most of its life more as a backdrop for wedding party photos than as a golf hole. The story goes that shortly after opening, Gary Player, Jack Nicklaus and Arnold Palmer were scheduled to play a Big Three match on the unique Trent Jones masterpiece. When they reached the third, however, Player couldn't negotiate the 250-yard carry and refused to play. The tee was taken out of commission for nearly 40 years, but was restored in early 2002. Regardless of the tee choice, this is Trent Jones' heroic-style architecture at its very best, with an order of intimidation on the side. With the surf crashing against the beds of black lava, players are asked to fly their Sunday-best punch into a crosswind to a huge green. The surface is two-tiered, meaning a long blast without precision easily results in a bogey.

261 YARDS

PAR 3

Medinah Country Club (No. 3)

Location: **Medinah, Ilinois**
Opened: **1928**
Architects: **Tom Bendelow (1928)/Harry Collis (1932)**
Par: **72**
Length: **7,401 yards**

There is something quintessentially American about Medinah Country Club and its No. 3 course. It is a foster kid of a golf course designed and redesigned time after time at a melting pot of a club. It has gone through endless tinkering, retooling, reworking and fiddling in its 75 years, revealing a restless dissatisfaction with the way things are that is so true to the country's nature. But through its regular makeovers, and all the attempts to elevate its ability to defend itself against the game's strongest players, it has become a fixture in American golf, a challenge of substance and consequence that frequently produces moments as uniquely American as the re-emergence of an old favorite and the coronation of a new hero, all in the midst of a gallery ready, willing and waiting for a high five.

Medinah No. 3 did not start out as a championship layout, though it was initially lauded as the most interesting of the three courses on site at the club, founded by Shriners and home to an incredible clubhouse that seems to be equal part Byzantine, Asian, Italianate and Louis XIV in architectural style. The No. 3 course, designed originally by Tom Bendelow, was to be the ladies' course. Bendelow's methods of course design have been attacked in the past as being limited, rushed and lifeless and, while much of that is pure personal opinion, it was a fact that the first time a tournament of substance was played on No. 3, the 1930 Medinah Open, Harry Cooper blitzed through the course with a 63.

From that moment began an overriding urge to bolster the No. 3 layout. Harry Collis was brought in, and his efforts produced five new holes and added length. The next time the tour players came through, in 1935, Cooper won again, but this time with a four-day total of five-over-par 289. Thus, the modus operandi for Medinah No. 3 was confirmed. No fewer than three other architects, George Fazio, Roger Packard and Roger Rulewich, have imposed their

The uncomfortable bend of the 11th hole is exacerbated by the omnipresent trees.

vision on refortifying Medinah for each of its major championships, and the result has been a course that remains a consistently formidable test, a classic American parkland layout playing through towering trees.

Aside from the holes where gaping Lake Kadijah sweeps into the landscape, largely the par-3 second, 13th and 17th holes, Medinah No. 3 is permeated by a sense of claustrophobia, a trait that is principally the result of the masses of trees lining fairway after fairway (reports indicate at least 6,000 have been planted on the site).

These trees are not merely scenery, however. They impact the strategy and line of many tee shots and more than a few second shots. They thwart the cutting off of doglegs and they make recovery possible only for the heroic. They are the primary defense at Medinah, an unyielding obstruction that compounds the challenge of its brutish 7,400 yards. While only a half-dozen or so of the holes have a substantial bend to them (most significant might be the 452-yard 16th), the overriding theme at Medinah No. 3 is the straightaway, straightforward par 4 through a boulevard of hardwoods (the 447-yard fourth is an exquisite example, where a fairway bunker is neither found nor needed). The No. 3 course is not a thrill ride or an adventure hike as much as it is a day of hard labor. It is blue collar and as mean as the wind in Chicago. It is not here to charm you. As the legendary sportswriter Jim Murray once put it, "If this course were human, it would be a prime suspect in the Sam Giancanca killing. Its nickname would be 'Machine Gun,' 'Baby Face' or 'Pretty Boy.' It should hang in every post office, or make the FBI's ten most-wanted list."

Feature Hole

The 17th typifies the trifling that has gone on at the No. 3 course for its entire existence. Changed at least three different times, it has gone from a stout three-wood par 3, to a goofy-greened one-shotter to its current state as a fair but fulsome shot to a green set well up a bank above Lake Kadijah. Bunkers hover into view well short of the green and the water isn't really in play either. The difficulty comes when the smallish green is missed and you find heavy rough. The hole was changed in preparation for the 1990 U.S. Open, but the five-percent grade on the green didn't work well with faster greens. So Roger Rulewich retooled the hole by moving the green 30 yards inland. Fittingly, the club has plans to move the green, bringing the water into play once again. But that's OK. Medinah is used to it by now.

206 YARDS

PAR 3

Trees, bunkers and even the flag pole make every aspect of the 18th hole seem cramped.

1949: Cary Middlecoff wins the first of his two U.S. Opens, defeating Sam Snead and Clayton Heafner by a shot. A Snead bogey at the 71st hole costs him a chance at the one title that eluded him his entire career.

1990: Hale Irwin, a 45-year-old veteran playing on a special exemption, rolls in a 45-foot birdie putt on the 72nd hole to force a tie with Mike Donald. Irwin wins the playoff to claim his third U.S. Open win.

DEFINING
MOMENTS

1975: Lou Graham, using a driver that he shortened by half-an-inch just days before the tournament, claims his only major championship, defeating John Mahaffey in a Monday play-off 71–73.

1999: Tiger Woods makes a gutsy par-saving putt on the 71st hole and fends off upstart Sergio Garcia to win PGA Championship, his second professional major title.

Even the green isn't a safe spot on the demanding 17th hole

Merion Golf Club (East)

Location: **Ardmore, Pennsylvania**
Opened: **1912**
Architect: **Hugh Wilson**
Par: **70**
Length: **6,544 yards**

Few if any objects on this earth, let alone golf courses, inspire such passions as the East Course at Merion Golf Club near Philadelphia. Tommy Armour, the legendary player and teacher, once romanticized, "If I had just two weeks to live, I'd want to go to Merion and play there every day." This is one of the great American golfing treasures, a place where Bobby Jones and Ben Hogan and Jack Nicklaus all triumphed. But it was Lee Trevino, who won his second U.S. Open in a playoff over Jack Nicklaus at Merion in 1971, whose passion overflowed. "Merion," he said, "I love her, and I don't even know her last name."

A quirky layout shoehorned amid the neighborhoods and traffic along Philadelphia's Main Line, Merion East is without fail a consummate test of the marriage between a player's mental and physical skills. How is such an immense challenge accomplished on such a small portion of land (barely 110 acres)? You could point to the bunkers. Merion's amateur architect Hugh Wilson, whose design career included not even a handful of other courses after Merion, managed to place every one of the course's 128 bunkers in a perfectly damning location. Wilson's bunkers, the famed "white faces of Merion," stand glaringly obvious as the hole lays out before the player, heightening the pre-shot anxiety.

Or you could point to the greens. Subtle and varied in size, each green is an ideal requirement for the length of hole attached to it. As Herbert Warren Wind once described, Merion's greens are "wonderfully varied-plateau greens, bench greens, crown greens, sunken greens, large greens, small greens, two-level greens, three-level greens and greens that slope in a hundred different directions."

Or you could point to the flow. Merion's sense of rhythm unfolds in an ever-increasing wave to a finish reserved for legends. Or maybe it's just this: that at every hole Merion exemplifies both the challenge, the difficulty and the reward of golf. In the words of George Fazio, "Merion has character. It is challenging without being backbreaking."

Indeed, as Trevino has said, you step to the first tee at Merion thinking par is surely the worst you can do. Quickly, however, you realize you are walking a tightrope above a pool of alligators for the next four hours. The first hole seems gentle enough, save for the nine bunkers that line every side of fairway and green. By the fourth hole, you have finished with the par 5s and while the next two holes are voracious par 4s (particularly the fifth where fairway and green both cant severely toward a stream) not once in the next five holes does the yardage exceed 375 yards. The delicate 13th is right in the neighborhood of Pine Valley's 10th hole and Pebble Beach's seventh among all-time-great short par 3s. The final five at Merion are the grandest of stuff, including a heroic

finish through an old quarry on Nos. 16 through 18.

The 16th and 18th are the two longest par 4s on the course, while the 17th is a 224-yard par 3. The final hole calls for a long drive to a plateaued fairway and then a long second to a plateaued green. Merion may have been toying with you at the start, but at the end it is all hard labor.

Merion is the great historic icon of American golf, a wondrous stage with fittingly unique props like its white sand, its scotch broom grass and its red wicker baskets atop every flagstick. Technology's effect on distance may have removed it as a valid test for the game's super-elite players, but for the rest of us, it remains a highly functional relic that challenges every aspect of our games. Says Pete Dye, "Merion asks the golfer to enjoy its classic beauty, but it demands his alertness, his golf knowledge, his courage and his finest ability."

1924: Bobby Jones dominates match play to win his first U.S. Amateur title, defeating Francis Ouimet 11 & 9 in the semi-final, and George Von Elm 9 & 8 in the final.

1950: Coming back from life-threatening injuries sustained in an automobile accident, Ben Hogan laces a majestic 1-iron to the 18th green at the U.S. Open. He makes his par and wins in a playoff over George Fazio and Lloyd Mangrum.

DEFINING MOMENTS

1930: Jones completes golf's Grand Slam with a win in the U.S. Amateur at Merion. He defeats Gene Homans in the final 8 & 7 with a crowd of 18,000 following the match.

1971: Lee Trevino and Jack Nicklaus square off in a playoff for the U.S. Open title. An epic contrast of styles, Trevino jokingly tosses a rubber snake at Nicklaus before the two begin the playoff, which Trevino wins 68–71.

Out of bounds left and bunkers everywhere make the 15th vexing.

Feature Hole

Whether you call the stream of Cobb's Creek that shortens the fairway and frames the green on this downhill hole the "Babbling Brook" or the "Baffling Brook," there is ample evidence to suggest this is one of the premier short par 4s in American golf. Former USGA executive director and PGA Tour Commissioner Joe Dey referred to the 11th as "the classic pitching hole." The drive is blind over a hill tumbling toward the water and, under normal conditions, players often will hit less than a driver off the tee here. Ideally, the second shot settles in the flatland before the brook, leaving a wedge to the green. A distracting bunker at the left front of the green further squeezes the narrow, throw-rug-sized green. Here is where Bobby Jones closed out his U.S. Amateur and Grand Slam-clinching match with Gene Homans in 1930. It has also been the site of numerous twos and a 12 made by 16-year-old Mason Rudolph in the 1950 U.S. Open.

370 YARDS

PAR 4

Muirfield Village Golf Club

Location: **Dublin, Ohio**
Opened: **1974**
Architect: **Jack Nicklaus and Desmond Muirhead**
Par: **72**
Length: **7,224 yards**

The prevailing wisdom regarding Muirfield Village is that it is to Jack Nicklaus what Augusta National was to Bobby Jones. Muirfield Village was originally conceived by Nicklaus as an opportunity to create a facility that would be ideal for golf spectating in addition to being a particularly inventive challenge for all levels of players. It is certainly manicured like Augusta National and the rolling fairways, sloping terrain and omnipresent streams remind you of the course that Bobby Jones first built in his native Georgia. But, from the outset, Nicklaus maintained the comparisons weren't valid. For instance, in *The Story of Muirfield Village,* he says, "The fact that I like Augusta National had nothing to do with the design of this course. This course is really a conglomerate of what's happened to me in my life and what the game of golf has meant to me."

Clearly, at Muirfield Village the attempt is not just to paint a pretty picture, though that certainly can be the case at holes like the watery par-3 12th, where the distant green shimmers off the pooling water. No, Muirfield Village's design demands performance in all phases of the game if it is to be survived. Indeed, even Nicklaus himself, the man who made a career by hitting the long, forceful, even risky shot, understood where the truth of the game resides.

"Golf to me is a game of precision more than power," Nicklaus said not long after its debut as the site of a tour event in the 1970s, "and I think the course reflects that."

What the course reflects more than anything is the perspective of a player playing the game and not merely an architect's theories. Even though designers Pete Dye, and especially Desmond Muirhead, contributed in the early stages of the planning, Nicklaus is at the root of everything, massaging the holes one way or another seemingly every year prior to the annual Memorial Tournament. Nicklaus emphasized the thrill of the possible in his design. That's why more

The 15th's tight lines reveal a par–5 that demands power and precision.

than two-thirds of the holes play downhill from elevated tees, and only two holes have uphill approaches. "Golf is a much better game played downhill," Nicklaus says, "and much more fun."

But Muirfield Village is not merriment without restriction. For instance, it is a golf course that rewards the high, long hit almost exclusively, as the number of genuine run-up greens can be counted on one hand. Eleven holes bring some degree of water in play and there are 71 bunkers, all as beautifully maintained as they are infuriatingly positioned. It is a wonderful orchestra of holes. For many players, four of the par 5s are reachable in two shots. But in every case, the punishment for wayward shots is swift and sufficient. The 15th, the shortest par 5, is narrow and guarded by a stream. The long par 4s (there are seven over 435 yards) are nearly equal-ly divided among straight shots, fades and draws off the tee.

But Muirfield Village's real treasure remains the short holes. Par 3s like the fourth invite trouble, while the eighth and 12th are noteworthy for being both the shortest and least merciful holes on the course. And the short par 4s, like the stream and pond-laden third and 14th holes, are among the course's most challenging and visually arresting.

Muirfield Village clearly reflects Nicklaus' approach to the game. To achieve success, power is used forcefully but selectively, and the judicious player always has opportunities. Perhaps that's why those who have won here include a spectrum that runs from Hale Irwin to Jack Nicklaus, from Justin Leonard to Tiger Woods. "From the player's standpoint, everything is well defined," Nicklaus says. "You know exactly where you have to go and what you have to do."

Feature Hole

14

For a man who, as a player, tended to have the ability to subdue so many courses with his power, Nicklaus' shining moments at Muirfield Village are often those emphasizing finesse, not bravado. A particularly fine-tuned example might be Muirfield Village's 14th, the shortest par 4 on the course by nearly 40 yards. Here, Nicklaus makes use of a stream that divides the fairway right at about the range where overly ambitious tee balls might land. But even an iron isn't totally safe here, as the creek also runs along the left edge for more than 35 yards before turning right across the fairway. Then, the creek sidles up the right-hand side, cutting in front of the sharply angled, narrow green, whose left-to-right slope can be particularly insidious. Though the hole is thought to be a legitimate birdie opportunity, it often ranks among the five most difficult on the course.

363 YARDS

PAR 4

A classic finishing hole, the downhill drive must contend with trees, bunkers and a stream.

1966: Nicklaus, intrigued at the possibility of bringing a big-time golf course and a big-time golf event back to his native Columbus, settles on a site, saying of the original 180-acre tract, "This is obviously it."

1976: Roger Maltbie posts a four-round total of even par and wins the inaugural Memorial Tournament, defeating Hale Irwin in a playoff.

2001: Tiger Woods wins his third straight Memorial Tournament, surging past Paul Azinger to win the event by seven shots, the largest margin of victory in the history of the tournament.

DEFINING MOMENTS

1992: Justin Leonard, who only missed seven fairways in six rounds of match play and had to rally from four-down to reach the semifinals, wins the U.S. Amateur 8&7 over Tom Scherrer in the final.

1998: The U.S. team, led by veterans Dottie Pepper and Juli Inkster, hold on to defeat the Europeans in the Solheim Cup matches, 16–12. Pepper and Inkster are involved in securing five points for the U.S. side.

National Golf Links of America

Location: **Southampton, New York**
Opened: **1909**
Architect: **C. B. Macdonald**
Par: **73**
Length: **6,873 yards**

There were earlier courses opened in America, to be sure. There even were earlier C.B. Macdonald courses, courses that went on to be bigger and bolder and which played host to more golf championships. But in a very real sense these first attempts at golf course architecture in America were not much more than tentative baby steps. Only after C.B. Macdonald had his way with 250 acres on the shore by Peconic Bay did America begin to get a sense of what great golf course design could be. What it saw then—and still sees today—at the National Golf Links of America is how a carefully shaped piece of land can yield strategy, subtlety and swagger in a setting unrivalled in golf.

After it opened, Macdonald seemingly tinkered with the course throughout the rest of his life, adding yet another flash of sand to this turn or that. As Michelangelo had the Sistine Chapel ceiling frescoes, as Frank Lloyd Wright had "Falling Water," so Macdonald had "the National."

It would be his lasting statement about the game's beauty and challenge. Still, even at the end he refused to be certain of its completeness. He once wrote more than 20 years after beginning construction on the National, "I am not confident that the course is perfect and beyond criticism today."

For all of its present character, the National started simply as Macdonald's attempt to bring the feel of some of the greatest links holes to America. In typical Macdonald fashion, he seemed to be saying, "Gentlemen, do not pretend to amuse yourself with other diversions. This place here, this is the game." Among the favorites were holes that reflected some of the enduring design elements of the Road Hole from the Old Course, the Redan par 3 at North Berwick, the Sahara from Royal St. George's and the Alps from Prestwick. But every hole, especially those that did not borrow explicitly from other famous designs, has the look and feel of a grand stage at the National with Peconic Bay shimmering

The National's epic challenge is stirring from any viewpoint, particularly from above.

in the background and the famed massive windmill dominating the stirring links-style landscape.

Macdonald presents optional routes on many holes (fairways on the windswept links are sometimes 75 yards wide), challenging the bold, talented player, while at the same time giving the more marginal golfer a fighting chance. He once explained, "I try not to make the course any harder, but to make it more interesting, never forgetting that 80 percent of the members of any golf club cannot on average drive more than 175 yards. So I always study to give them their way out by taking a course such as a yachtsman does against an adverse wind, by tacking." And tacking is an important skill at the National where sand hazards are everywhere, some counting as many as 500 individual bunkers on the course.

Another thrill is the greens, full, wondrously wavy affairs with contours inventive in ways only an artist and tactician could appreciate. (Macdonald once said he dropped handfuls of pebbles on a diagram of a green and let the various piles determine where he should put his contours.)

But perhaps his greatest turn at the National is that he did not merely replicate great holes. Instead, he captured the feel of the challenge of certain elements of design. Through intense study of the best courses (to say nothing of his fascination with turf management), Macdonald understood how various design elements like diagonal hazards, green contours and sizes, and even the occasional forced carry among many others could and should work together. The National was not merely Macdonald at the height of his powers, it was golf course architecture at the height of its powers.

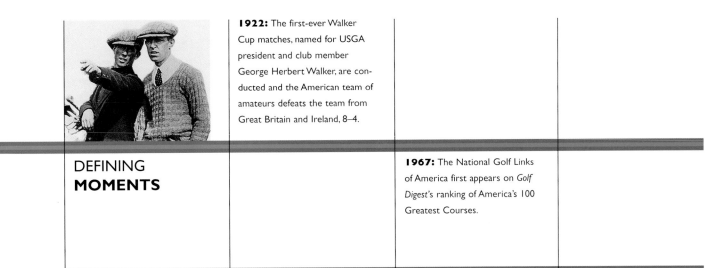

1922: The first-ever Walker Cup matches, named for USGA president and club member George Herbert Walker, are conducted and the American team of amateurs defeats the team from Great Britain and Ireland, 8–4.

DEFINING
MOMENTS

1967: The National Golf Links of America first appears on *Golf Digest's* ranking of America's 100 Greatest Courses.

Tucked to one side of the National's famed windmill is the punchbowl green on No. 16.

Feature Hole

17

From the tee of the hole named Peconic after the bay it overlooks, the player stands looking downhill at a fairway clouded in so much random sand that it appears to be riddled with the after-effects of a bombing run. There is a bold line over mounded dunes to the right, but even with an iron or fairway wood off the tee, there is more than a measure of uncertainty at the proper line. Indeed, the safer the route taken off the tee, the less sure the view of the green for the approach. Interestingly, the 17th was worked on by Macdonald a good 20 years after the National opened. He added 30 yards to the hole and increased the severity of the bunkering. As Robert Trent Jones once explained, holes like the 17th "demonstrate Macdonald's mastery of the strategic values of the links abroad that he revered."

368 YARDS

PAR 4

Oak Hill Country Club (East)

Location: **Rochester, New York**
Opened: **1926**
Architects: **Donald Ross/Robert Trent Jones Sr.**
(1955), George & Tom Fazio (1976)
Par: **71**
Length: **7,098 yards**

The East Course at Oak Hill Country Club is a conundrum. At once it is routinely lauded as one of Donald Ross' finest works, and yet it may also be one of his most distorted. And while Ross was of the mind that long courses were boring, today Oak Hill stretches out well over 7,000 yards, five football fields longer than Ross' original plan. Finally and most pointedly, Ross once suggested that trees had "a limited place" in golf and his original site at Oak Hill had only a modicum of trees. Today there may now be in excess of 40,000 trees on site, every single one of them planted after Ross had completed his work.

Oak Hill may not be what Ross had envisioned physically today, but its record has proven it to be a consummate test of golf played at the highest level. Fittingly, it is the combination of Ross' design with the majesty of its later plantings and the accumulated alterations over time that make Oak Hill a thriving example of American golf course architecture.

Debate its present looks as you see fit, there is no denying that Oak Hill is one of the great driving courses in golf. Fairways, especially for championship play, often can be reduced to as little as 23 yards wide. While not littered with an overwhelming number of fairway bunkers and hazards (11 of the 14 driving holes have some form of disruption in play), Oak Hill's forests of trees squeeze the outside edges of the fairways and can block the route to the green if those drives are off line. Plus, its heavily bunkered greens require a player to carefully choose his line of attack, starting with the placement of the tee ball.

Oak Hill establishes its tone early and with resonance. The first hole, once called by Ben Hogan "the toughest starting hole in golf," runs 460 yards straightaway with a bunker on the left side forcing action off the tee toward the right and out of bounds. The message is clear, says Rochester native,

The par–3 15th
is surrounded
by trouble.

Oak Hill member and former PGA Champion Jeff Sluman. "You don't get any warm-up holes. You've got to be ready once you step up on the first tee."

Nine of Oak Hill's par 4s are longer than 430 yards and, while downslopes in some of the landing areas can give accurate drivers 30 or more yards of roll, second shots into the greens need to be especially precise. One of Oak Hill's natural features that originally intrigued Ross was the meandering Allen's Creek, which affects play to varying degrees on eight different holes. It is especially nettlesome on the meaty 460-yard seventh, where the water cuts close on the right side and then slides across the middle of the fairway.

Over the years some of Ross' original good intentions have been misplaced. Robert Trent Jones Sr., a native of Rochester, added 300 yards or so and removed about 80

Ross bunkers that were largely no longer in play. Then, 20 years later, George and Tom Fazio, solved a traffic congestion problem during major championships by completely revamping the fifth and sixth holes. What has been touched relatively little is the strapping finish of 16, 17 and 18. Three par 4s each 20 yards longer than its predecessor, starting with the 439-yard 16th hole, followed by the par-5 17th (converted to a par 4 during championship play) and finishing with the now 480-yard 18th hole.

But for Joe Dey, the course went beyond the yardages and the numbers in its book. Said Dey, "Oak Hill is anything but a three-hole course. It is remarkable in its variety as a test of golf, as well as its beauty. The two features of variety and beauty are linked. Oak Hill's trees are lovely to behold and devilish to be behind."

Feature Hole

13

This is Oak Hill's memorial tribute hole, where a forest of trees behind the green honors great players and great men in the club's history. The legendary Hill of Fame's honorees include winners of major championships at Oak Hill, including Jack Nicklaus (1980 PGA), Lee Trevino (1968 U.S. Open) and Charlie Coe (1949 U.S. Amateur). The hole itself is interrupted by Allen's Creek at the 300-yard mark, so players will tee off with something less than a driver. The interrupting creek also prevented any player from reaching the green in two shots in the club's first 75 years of existence. Sturdy trees overhang the fairway in several spots along the hole, including at the final bend about 100 yards short of the green. But the putting surface is receptive to the short iron approaches and the long hole provides one of the few birdie chances on the back nine.

594
YARDS

PAR 5

The 18th green is set up on a hill, enhancing the brute strength of the finisher.

1956: Cary Middlecoff survives the final three holes to win his second U.S. Open by a single shot after Ben Hogan three-putts the 17th hole. "Those last three holes nearly killed us all," said Middlecoff.

1968: Lee Trevino wins his first PGA Tour title and first major at the U.S. Open by outplaying Bert Yancey and Jack Nicklaus with a final-round 69. He becomes the first player ever to shoot all four rounds in the 60s at a U.S. Open.

1995: Trailing by two points entering the final day's play, the European side wins seven-and-a-half points to defeat the U.S. 14½–13½ in a stunning upset at the Ryder Cup.

DEFINING
MOMENTS

1989: Curtis Strange wins his second straight U.S. Open by shooting a final-round 70 to upstage Tom Kite who led the field by three shots early in the final round only to stumble home with a 78.

The uphill 17th may look serene, but its bunkers and green make it a killer.

Oakland Hills Country Club (South)

Location: **Bloomfield Hills, Michigan**
Opened: **1918/1950**
Architects: **Donald Ross (1918)/Robert Trent Jones Sr. (1950)**
Par: **72**
Length: **7,105 yards**

Oakland Hills South Course, that one-time Donald Ross design usurped and transmogrified by Robert Trent Jones, stands as a resounding sea change in the history of American golf course architecture. It was here in the middle of the 20th century that the game began its eventual, inexorable transformation from a contest conducted via the bounce and the roll to an aerial exercise that demanded relentless precision to narrowly defined targets.

There's little doubt that the way the South Course plays today bears only a faded resemblance to the way Ross saw and designed the course in the second decade of the 20th century. But what Ross first saw then remains true, despite whatever revisions have been made over the years. Ross initially wrote of the land, "I rarely find a piece of property so well-suited for golf."

What Jones saw when he came to it three decades later wasn't so much a decline in the vivid setting as an unwanted acceleration in the progress of the game and its players. "The game had outrun architecture," he later explained.

Inspired by that assessment and with working orders to "make the course so tough that no one can win," Jones set about the business of revitalizing Ross' work in preparation for the 1951 U.S. Open. What he produced was the prototype for golf course architecture for the better part of the remainder of the 20th century. It was target golf to the fairway followed by target golf to the green.

The brute, which came to be known as "The Monster" during the week of the 1951 U.S. Open, was a startling combination of Ross' original routing and dramatically contoured greens—Jones admired them so, calling them "uniquely his and uniquely great"—with Jones' Dr Frankenstein-like enhancement of the challenge, what he termed hitting "clearly defined but well-defended landing areas." He added dozens of bunkers, removing many of Ross' original fairway traps, now too short. Further exacerbating the challenge, Jones pinched the fairways in the landing area with bunkers on both sides so that the landing areas routinely might be no more than 20 yards wide. Then, he set about fortifying every green with sentinels of sand, forcing players to approach the greens with soft, high shots.

The examples of Jones' imprint are clear right from the beginning where bunkers squeeze the landing area at Nos. 1, 2, 4 and 8. Elsewhere, the wildly original bunker on the 15th hole that blotches the middle of the fairway is a clear indication of Jones forcing his will upon the player. But there is enough of the original Ross design still in play, like the memorable 220-yard par-3 ninth and the infamous pond guarding both the 16th fairway and green. And the long 18th, routinely converted to a par 4 for championship play, stands as the quintessential finishing hole and the perfect melding of Jones' demands and Ross' famed contours.

Ben Hogan, in the locker room after completing play in that 1951 U.S. Open, is said to have referred to bringing "this course, this monster to its knees." Jones relished that, but, he later said, "The most satisfying thing about Oakland Hills was that at the end of the tournament, the great players' names were at the top of the leaderboard. To me, that was the real proof of the honest character of the layout." Honest or a monster? Oakland Hills South is both.

1937: Ralph Guldahl wins the U.S. Open, the first of two in a row, by two shots over Sam Snead, becoming the first player to post four straight under-par rounds to win the tournament.

1951: Ben Hogan challenges the Robert Trent Jones-refortified layout for the U.S. Open, and his sterling final round of 67, including a back-nine 32, helps him to a two-shot win over Clayton Heafner.

1972: Gary Player, making a miraculous birdie from the heavy rough over a tree and a pond on the 16th hole, claims his second PGA title. Player flew a 9-iron 150 yards over a willow tree that landed just four feet from the hole.

DEFINING **MOMENTS**

1979: David Graham wins the PGA Championship, the so-called "Massacre of the Monster" where the normally brutal South Course yielded 140 even-par or better rounds during the week.

1996: Tied playing the 18th hole on Sunday, Steve Jones beats Tom Lehman with a closing par on the brutal final hole. Lehman's tee ball bounded crazily into a fairway bunker giving him no shot of reaching the green.

Bunkers dictate play both off the tee and to the 18th green.

Feature Hole

16

At first glance the aerial assault nature of the 16th hole might lead you to believe it was manufactured by Robert Trent Jones during his redesign of Oakland Hills for the 1951 U.S. Open. The fact is, however, that the hole is largely the province of the original architect Donald Ross. The hole remains typical Ross, a classic use of a natural feature. Ross put the pond very much in play for both the drive and the approach (indeed, the slightly downhill tee shot is often played with 3-wood or long iron), and he perched the green on the very edge of the water, too. Gary Player's blind second from the rough and over the willows stopped four feet from the stick to give him a crucial birdie in his 1972 PGA Championship win. Jones called the 16th simply "the most spectacular and the most difficult on the course."

406 YARDS PAR 4

Oakmont Country Club

Location: **Oakmont, Pennsylvania**
Opened: **1904**
Architect: **Henry and William Fownes**
Par: **70**
Length: **6,946 yards**

From its very beginnings, when the par for the course was set at 80, Oakmont Country Club has made no apologies and taken no prisoners. It prides itself on being a brutal test of golf from tee to green, seemingly laughing full-throated at the visiting golfer like an evil genie. It was, according to 1927 U.S. Open winner Tommy Armour, "a cruel and treacherous playground." It still is. Par may no longer be 80 at Oakmont, but it sure feels like it.

Oakmont defines penal architecture in the way a sigmoidoscopy defines invasive procedure. Every inch of its layout appears specifically orchestrated to exhaust the will of the golfer. And while William Fownes, the son of Oakmont's original developer, architect and president Henry Fownes, spent many years adding to the course's challenge, its true mission has never changed. It was William who best espoused the design philosophy at Oakmont when he said, "A shot poorly played should be a shot irrevocably lost."

The aim of the father, and later the son, was for their piece of golf property to reflect the genuine origins of the game on links land. So Henry Fownes had his crew cut down nearly every tree on the property before they began laying out any golf holes. What resulted was a place at once desolate yet invigorating. Though its middle years marred the landscape with flora and made Oakmont appear almost pleasant, recent efforts by the club to restore its cold feel have resulted in the removal of nearly 2,000 trees. Once again, the course has the beastly visage that Herbert Warren Wind once summarized thus: "Oakmont is not a pretty course. But then, a pretty Oakmont would be incongruous. It is not intended to arouse feelings of warmth and affection."

No, rather like a military training base's obstacle course, Oakmont is a series of hurdles that induce fear, exact pain and in the end may produce quiet, fatigued exhilaration. The holes pound away at you here. Oakmont starts with a

There are no shortcuts at Oakmont, particularly on its long par–4 finisher.

beastly par 4 of 483 yards with the second shot downhill to a green sloping away from the player. This isn't a wake-up call from the front desk; it's Reveille played in your eardrum. The beat, of course, goes on. There's the famous 60-yard long, 30-yard wide Church Pews bunker catching pulls and hooks on the third and fourth holes, the 253-yard one-shotter on No. 8 with its 100-yard bunker on the right side, the blind uphill drive on the 481-yard ninth and its 100-yard-long green, and the long uphill par 4s at 15 and 18 to complete the comminution. While Oakmont is relentless, it doesn't get in a rut. Nifty, short par 4s like the fifth, 14th and the driveable 17th, while no less exacting, offer just a glimmer of hope. Oakmont exercises its power with staggeringly little use of water hazards and only minimal out-of-bounds. Again, its principal weapon is the sand, and it is everywhere.

In fact, 10 of its 14 par 4s and par 5s have bunkers on both sides of their fairways, and every green but the 18th is guarded by at least three sand pits.

But as vexing as the sand can be at Oakmont, its final line of defense is its most taxing. The greens are lightning quick, perhaps the most fearsome in championship golf, and firm. Oakmont demands excellence simply for survival, and its greatest tribute might be that the best have always played and won there. More U.S. major golf titles have been contested at Oakmont (15) than anywhere else. Bobby Jones, Gene Sarazen, Sam Snead, Ben Hogan and Jack Nicklaus all have major titles at Oakmont. None of them probably loved it very much, but all respected it the way Jones did, who once said, "It was, and is, a severe golf course, the best test of championship golf in this country."

Feature Hole

3

Bad shots at Oakmont are punished, often severely. That is the philosophy at Oakmont and that is most certainly the philosophy of Oakmont's gaping, but eye-catching, hazard just left of the landing area between the third and fourth fairways. Nicknamed the "Church Pews" bunker, it is a near-football-field-sized collection basket of sand, separated by eight strips of grass mounding, each rising three feet above the sand. Separating the third and fourth fairways, the Church Pews comes into play for tee shots hit to the left on both holes. It becomes especially nasty on the third where a trio of bunkers also guards the right side of the fairway and the second shot plays uphill to a green that slopes away from the player. Tom Watson once said of the troublesome trap, "That is why they call it the Church Pews. You pray that you can get the hell out of that thing."

426 YARDS

PAR 4

The 14th is shrouded by a dozen bunkers, but the biggest stand watch around the green.

1927: Oakmont holds up well in playing host to its first U.S. Open. Not a single player in the field breaks 300 for the four rounds, and Tommy Armour wins in a next-day playoff, firing a 76 to Harry Cooper's 79.

1962: Jack Nicklaus wins his first tournament, and his first major as a professional, defeating local hero Arnold Palmer in a playoff, 71–74.

DEFINING MOMENTS

1953: Ben Hogan wins the second leg of his triumvirate of major titles in 1953, finishing at five under par for the week, six shots clear of Sam Snead.

1973: Johnny Miller rebounds from a potentially disastrous third round 76 to set a new U.S. Open scoring record of 63. It still stands as the lowest final round ever posted by the winner of a major.

Olympia Fields Country Club (North)

Location: **Olympia Fields, Illinois**
Opened: **1922**
Architect: **Willie Park**
Par: **70**
Length: **7,177 yards**

I t is fitting that the first president of Olympia Fields Country Club was the legendary football coach Amos Alonzo Stagg, the inventor of the tackling dummy. The truth about Olympia Fields' beefy North Course is that it is nothing more and nothing less than 7,000 yards of cross body blocks, end-arounds and clothesline tackles.

Originally the North Course was the fourth 18-hole layout at the Club, whose membership rolls at the time had swelled to nearly 1,200. Designed by two-time British Open champion Willie Park Jr., whose resume includes such notables as Sunningdale in England and Maidstone on Long Island, the North was the premier layout of the four and immediately became one of the most respected championship courses in the country. In its first two decades of existence, no fewer than nine major golf championships were played there, including two PGA Championships, two NCAA Championships, a U.S. Open and two Western Opens, then one of the major titles in golf. Continually, the course itself dominated the proceedings. Scores like 10 over in the 1928 U.S. Open were good enough for the final-round lead. Even in recent times, a refortified Olympia Fields North has held its own, as Graham Marsh's winning score in the 1997 U.S. Senior Open remained at even par.

"I don't think this is a golf course that you can go after and attack," Marsh said in 1997.

Framed by trees, studded with elevation change and interrupted on occasion by ponds and Butterfield Creek, Olympia Fields North is sturdy stuff, even by Chicago standards. It starts out like a midwestern football powerhouse's offensive line, with holes of 580, 471 and 461 yards. And then the trees start pinching the fairways. During the 1997

The water on the 18th goes from adornment to vexation the minute a drive ends up off the fairway.

U.S. Senior Open, fully nine of the North's holes cracked the list of the top-50 hardest holes on the Senior PGA Tour.

From the back tees, there is not a par 4 on the front nine shorter than 400 yards, and one of the par 3s is the 247-yard eighth, which plays slightly uphill and into the wind to a green with only a narrow opening in front. There is more of the same on the back nine, but the most trying holes might be the shortest. The par-3 13th has a large, undulating green and the uphill tee shot encourages a pull into trouble on the left, while the par-4 12th, which skirts around bunkers, the stream and then calls for a precise approach, can be especially nasty. The 14th is no slouch either, playing 444 yards to a plateaued green above the stream.

At Olympia Fields trees can seem like blitzing linebackers, especially on holes like the fourth, where a stand of trees blocking the right side of the fairway seemingly directs your tee shot into a deep fairway bunker on the left. Even tee shots only slightly pulled or pushed can clip an overhanging branch and drop straight down in to the deep rough. It can be more than a little frustrating to find the treeline at Olympia Fields. Says Dave Stockton: "If you put it in the rough, then you have to get it up, but you're under trees, so you can't get it up because you'll hit the trees above your head."

Without question, Olympia Fields North can be a grinding marathon, especially with the length and bunkering recently added by architect Mark Mungeam. Its requirements are as simple and direct as a running back's stiff-arm to the facemask. As Marsh said in 1997: "Part of the game on this golf course is just not making bogeys."

1925: Walter Hagen wins his second PGA Championship by playing 175 holes in five matches on his way to a 6&5 victory over Bill Melhorn. Hagen had earlier defeated Al Watrous in 39 holes and Leo Diegel in 40.

1928: Johnny Farrell hands Bobby Jones his third runner-up finish in five years at the U.S. Open. Farrell wins by a stroke in a 36-hole playoff after both players finished regulation at ten-over par 294.

1997: Australian Graham Marsh wins his first major championship, defeating John Bland by a single shot at the U.S. Senior Open. Marsh finishes at even par 280 with a closing birdie and a par on the final two holes.

DEFINING **MOMENTS**

1961: Jerry Barber holes three monstrous putts of 20, 40 and 60 feet in the final three holes to force a playoff with Don January in the PGA Championship. Barber wins the playoff the next day, shooting 67 to January's 68.

If the 444-yard 10th hole isn't imposing enough, just look back at the mammoth 80-foot clubhouse clocktower.

Feature Hole

14

Olympia Fields has its burly moments, but few as burly as the 14th hole with its dramatic natural elevation change, water in play and a green with an attitude. Butterfield Creek works its way across the fairway twice , framing the landing area and forcing the exceptionally long hitters to gear down or risk reaching the back end of the water with their downhill tee shots. Of course, the idea is to get as close to the stream as possible off the tee so that your second shot, which climbs back uphill to the green, is a little less arduous. Players will routinely have 150–175 yards to a green guarded by three bunkers. Bobby Jones, defeated by Johnny Farrell in a 36-hole playoff at Olympia Fields in the 1928 U.S. Open, had high praise for the 14th, which he and others called "the valley of decision." "It ranks among the finest in my selection of great golf holes," he said.

444 YARDS

PAR 4

Peachtree Golf Club

Location: **Atlanta, Georgia**
Opened: **1947**
Architect: **Robert Trent Jones and Bobby Jones**
Par: **72**
Length: **7,043 yards**

There are only two golf courses that Bobby Jones helped design. One was Augusta National, and its place among golf's great cathedrals was secure from the day it opened. Atlanta's Peachtree is the other, and equally great things were expected of it. (Indeed, some in Georgia referred to the project as "Augusta National West.")

Golf courses, not unlike younger siblings, suffer from comparison to their more established precursors, though. So it is not fair to suggest Peachtree is like Augusta National. Nevertheless, an argument can be made that Peachtree is at least as historically significant as Augusta. The reason? Because here at Peachtree, Trent Jones unveiled the type of heroic architecture that would come to be his calling card, a card that would be accepted and endorsed worldwide.

Trent admitted as much himself, writing in *Golf's Magnificent Challenge*, "Often it is difficult to pinpoint the event that launches a career, or at least accelerates it. For me the moment is relatively easy to define. Peachtree did it."

Peachtree came to exemplify the sort of long aerial-challenge game that, Trent Jones felt, modern equipment and modern players necessitated. Here, he brought in his new favorite line of defense against technology and talent, namely the water hazard. There are 11 ponds at Peachtree and water is on view on 14 holes. But it does not make every hole it touches at Peachtree a punishment. Trent clearly listened when Bobby, himself tired of five- and six-hour rounds, warned him during the construction that "water is to a sand trap what an airplane accident is to an automobile accident. You can't recover from one, but you might from the other." Water only really becomes especially intimidating at half a dozen holes, most notably the 524-yard second with its greenside, fairway-splitting pond and the par-5 10th and 16th, where the stream crosses the fairway right where layup shots may land.

The large multilevel green on the 18th hole is typical Jones and typical Peachtree.

But Trent was thinking well beyond the championship-level player, too. It was at Peachtree that Jones began perfecting two elements of his architectural paradigm, and each, in its own way, was an attempt to accommodate and challenge a wide spectrum of playing abilities. First, Jones built long runway-style teeboxes at Peachtree that sometimes stretched forward for 80 yards. The idea was to equate the ability of all players to carry the proper line and land in the proper spot off the tee, regardless of how far they hit their drivers. Second, Jones fitted Peachtree with large, often multi-tiered putting surfaces. The theory was that there could be as many as ten different hole locations on these large greens. The mammoth undulating putting surfaces (they averaged 8,000 square feet and the 10th was more than 10,000 square feet, among the largest in American golf at the time) meant players of moderate ability could hit them more easily. Players of supreme ability would have to be especially exacting to hit the proper portion of the greens.

Throughout the constantly changing elevation of the property at Peachtree, there is a hint of Bobby Jones' more famous home course two hours east in Augusta (like the National, it too was a former nursery). And the flashing of the bunkering, the impact of the water hazards and the contouring of the greens has an Augusta National feel but Peachtree stands apart as the seminal Trent Jones original design, particularly for the man himself.

"I still believe," Jones later wrote, "that the course set a standard for modern golf course architecture. Certainly its features have been incorporated into countless courses, mine as well as others."

Feature Hole

14

If the belief is that Peachtree is in its way an imitation of Augusta National, it is because holes like No. 14 give the notion legs. Put together in much the same way Trent Jones reconfigured the 16th hole at Augusta, Peachtree's 14th is the sort of par 3 Jones devised simply as a test of one's golfing courage. The bailout area right of the green and even the accompanying bunkers seem to slope toward the water, which guards the entire left and front edges of the green. The water's impact on the hole increases with one's ability to challenge it. If Jones' philosophy of golf holes could be summed up by the overused but accurate phrase "hard par, easy bogey," then the 14th reflects that challenge. You can play the 14th for the hole and be in the water. You can play the 14th safe, but you will not be close to the hole.

179 YARDS

PAR 3

Those who want to compare Peachtree to Augusta National have ample evidence.

1945: Bobby Jones organizes a group of Atlantans to embark on a new golf club, telling the group of businessmen, "I would like your support, so I'll need a check for $100,000 apiece from you by next Monday morning."

1967: Sam Snead defeats Julius Boros (below) in a Shell's Wonderful World of Golf match. The filming takes two days so spectators are told to wear the same clothes when they come back for the second day.

DEFINING
MOMENTS

1989: The Great Britain and Ireland side wins the last hole of the last match to claim the Walker Cup on U.S. soil for the first time in the history of the competition.

Pebble Beach Golf Links

Location: **Pebble Beach, California**
Opened: **1919**
Architects: **Jack Neville and Douglas Grant**
Par: **72**
Length: **6,841 yards**

Pebble Beach's epic conclusion begins with the 17th hole and its hourglass green.

I s Pebble Beach a happy accident or a grand gift to golf from the creative genius of man? Is it natural wonder or magical manufacturing? Is it cathedral or playground? It is unquestionably an American treasure, an icon of golf course architecture that is so intensely tied to its setting that its holes cannot be thought of, in any way, as being found anywhere else. Pebble Beach is entirely its setting. Nothing more, nothing less. That is its genius. That is its allure. That is its indelible imprint on golf in America.

The case for Pebble Beach is made most strongly by a more than reliable source. Jack Nicklaus, winner of national titles there as both an amateur and a professional, once wrote, "It is my favorite place on earth to play golf. It is partly the location, as dramatic as any course in the country, but mostly it is the complete test of golf it presents." Indeed, Pebble Beach presents backdrops like 50-cent postcards at every turn, but it is also an extreme inquisition of all the important facets of a well-rounded golf game. It is difficult stances, difficult decisions, difficult lines and angles and interpretations of options. And, oh by the way, just try hitting its dinner plate-sized greens.

Yet despite the rigors of its requirements and the distractions of its tableau, Pebble Beach is never an inappropriate test. Not once do you feel unfairly accosted by holes that ask too much or give too little. It starts simply but thoughtfully with a par 4 that makes you think of working the ball right out of the box. It lets you play your way into the course, waiting just long enough for you to get ready for its best.

Then, at the uphill par-5 sixth hole, the grandeur of Pebble Beach that you have been expecting takes hold. Here, and through the next four holes, can be found the most thorough collection of ocean-side golf shots as can be experienced anywhere. A player's biggest, best drives are called for at holes six, eight, nine and 10, where the threat of pushing a ball to the right into the ocean is very real on the latter three holes. Yet, interspersed amid this length (the par 4s together add up to well over 1,300 yards) are tricky half shots like the third at the sixth and certainly the tee shot to the microscopic green at the downhill par-3 seventh hole.

While the course moves inland again, the holes are not to be overlooked. The greens throughout are tiny placemats with breaks that only the veteran caddies can see. Especially noteworthy might be the big-hearted par-5 14th with its gaping front bunker, which can make the simplest of wedge approach shots nightmarish.

The course returns to the sea in dramatic fashion with the final two holes, the long par-3 17th, where both Nicklaus and Tom Watson performed feats of magic in winning U.S. Opens in 1972 and '82. The closer is an American legend, a

par 5 marching up the coastline, surf crashing against the rocks, distracting the player on each of his three shots, or two if he's especially bold.

Pebble Beach has changed occasionally over the years, the most important work being done by Chandler Egan who reworked greens and bunkers and most importantly lengthened the 18th into a classic par 5 in the late 1920s, in preparation for the U.S. Amateur in 1929. But its character was there right from the beginning and remains to this day. "It was all there in plain sight," the original architect Jack Neville remembers. "The big idea was to get in as many holes as possible along the bay. It took a little imagination, but not much. Years before it was built I could see Pebble Beach as a golf links. Nature had intended that it be nothing else."

1929: The U.S. Amateur is held west of the Rockies for the first time, and the two-time defending champion Bobby Jones is eliminated in the first round. Harrison "Jimmy" Johnston wins the title over Dr. O.F. Willing.

1947: Bing Crosby decides to relocate his successful celebrity pro-am golf tournament to the Monterey Peninsula, where it remains to this day.

1961: Jack Nicklaus completes his amateur career with his second U.S. Amateur title, crushing Dudley Wysong in the final 8&6. For the week, Nicklaus is estimated to be 24-under par in the 136 holes he played.

2000: Tiger Woods wins his first U.S. Open crown in obliterating fashion. Woods equals the all-time U.S. Open scoring record of 272, finishes at a record-setting 12-under par and wins by an unheard of 15 shots.

DEFINING MOMENTS

1972: For the first time, the U.S. Open is contested at Pebble Beach and Nicklaus expands on his Monterey Peninsula success by winning the title with a glorious 1-iron to two inches at the 71st hole.

Feature Hole

8

Picking a favorite hole at Pebble Beach is the kind of task usually reserved for late-night discussions by the slightly overserved on a golf trip. But perhaps it is best to rely on the wisdom of Jack Nicklaus, who won two national titles at Pebble Beach (and nearly a third). Nicklaus called the approach on the eighth hole over a cliff and across a rousing inlet to a green hanging on the edge of disaster, simply "the greatest second shot in golf." It is that and more. From the tee, players face a blind uphill shot, then must fly the ocean with their second. The only thing more staggering than the view is the challenge. The hole really developed its teeth after Alister Mackenzie repositioned the green closer to the edge and then sloped it gently, but diabolically, toward the water.

418 YARDS

PAR 4

The long 6th, tiny 7th and grand 8th are completely natural and completely perfect holes.

Pinehurst Resort & Country Club (No. 2)

Location: **Pinehurst, North Carolina**
Opened: **1907/1925/1935**
Architect: **Donald Ross**
Par: **71**
Length: **7,189 yards**

When you come to the first tee at Pinehurst No. 2, there is no visual cue that you are embarking on greatness. There is no overwhelming sense of grandeur, no cascading surf, no looming mountain scapes, no epic vistas. It is mostly quaint, uniquely quiet and comfortably still. Pinehurst No. 2 may not announce its glory to all who enter it, but surely, in the course of their tour of the confines, they will come to know its particularly special and exacting challenges. It may not be overtly great, but innately, intuitively, Pinehurst No. 2 exudes majesty. You may not see it at the start, but you will feel it by the time you finish.

In all cases, No. 2 fully meets Ross' intended mission, namely, "Golfers of every caliber will find in the No. 2 Course the fairest, yet most exacting, test of their game, and yet a test from which they will always derive the maximum amount of pleasure."

Only those ready to be tested will truly get that much pleasure from Ross' masterpiece, however. Generally speaking, Pinehurst No. 2 does not assault the player's ability to execute the tee shot. Truthfully, to be successful, the better player must position a tee shot in the correct half of the fairway to attack a championship pin position (the longish 11th hole is a perfect example, with its pinching fairway bunker in the distance on the left). But never is there an all-or-nothing proposition from the tee. There is only one water hazard on the entire course (at the start of the 16th hole), and provided you are playing the correct tees, it is, at most, only a minor concern.

No. 2's crowned, turtle-backed greens—and the player's approach to them—are the thing here. As Ross indicated, "Competitors whose second shots have wandered a bit will

The 9th hole provides some relief until a stray shot finds one of its six bunkers.

be disturbed by these apparently innocent slopes and by the shot they will have to invent to recover."

Beyond the greens, No. 2 presents a wondrous stage to concentrate on the game. Every hole is framed by stately pines, yet stray shots are often easily retrieved and one does at least have the chance of comfortably putting the ball back into play. The rhythm mixes in just the right amount of finesse holes, like the third and the seventh on the front nine, each less than 405 yards, each guarded by more than the average number of sand traps and waste bunkers. Those, of course, are balanced out by monumental challenges at the long fifth and eighth, the latter playing nearly 490 yards as a par 4, the second shot is decidedly uphill to a green fashioned like an upside-down soup tureen.

The back-and-forth nature of the course continues on the back nine, building to a fittingly stout finish on the final four holes. The 15th is a dastardly long par 3. The 16th often plays in competition as a monstrous par 4 to a green protected by six bunkers. The downhill par-3 17th almost provides a respite, before the surge up 18, an uphill par 4 where every miss from tee to green is punished. But in typical Ross fashion, and especially at Pinehurst No. 2, the penalty is not often deadly, as Payne Stewart proved with his par-save to win the U.S. Open in 1999.

Pinehurst is no mere affectation; its challenge is decidedly straightforward. As was once said by Tom Watson, "There's nothing tricky about Pinehurst No. 2. There are no blind shots on the entire course. Every hole shows you what you have to do. You have to just go out and do it." And in golf, that is pure greatness.

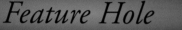

Feature Hole

The fifth is so typical of the occasional infuriation that Donald Ross chose to exact at the No. 2 course. A long par 4 that moves ever so deceptively up at the start and then slopes gently down to the green looks to be nothing other than long from the tee. But the fairway cants to match the dogleg to the left, and the green is then elevated with dropoffs to the left, just where the most likely miss is to occur. As Pinehurst's director of golf, Don Padgett, says, the fifth's green is like an inverted saucer that has "had the edges ground off." Getting on the green is no relief either, as the fifth might be No. 2's toughest putting test, as nearly two-thirds of green is sloped too severely to house a pin position. At the 1999 U.S. Open, it played as the toughest hole for the week with a 4.549 stroke average.

483 YARDS

PAR 4

The uphill par-3 15th starts a long, exacting finish at Pinehurst.

1936: A year after Ross converts the sand greens at the No. 2 course to grass, the PGA Championship is held there and Denny Shute defeats Jimmy Thomson in the 36-hole final, 3&2.

1951: Only two of the 12 matches played reached the final hole and the Americans rout the Great Britain and Ireland team 9½–2½ in the ninth Ryder Cup Matches.

1999: Payne Stewart makes a 15-foot putt on the 72nd hole to edge Phil Mickelson by a stroke and win the U.S. Open. It is the last title of 42-year-old Stewart's career, as he dies in a plane accident in October of that year.

DEFINING MOMENTS

1940: After seven years of futility, Ben Hogan wins the first title of his professional career, defeating Sam Snead by three shots at the North and South Open at Pinehurst No. 2.

At the 17th, like everywhere else at Pine Valley, any miss is certain death.

Pine Valley Golf Club

Location: **Pine Valley, New Jersey**
Opened: **1918**
Architect: **George Crump and H.S. Colt**
Par: **70**
Length: **6,667 yards**

Pine Valley is malice aforethought, yet all who play it revel in its malevolence. Only a truly special golf course can make you love it as it unleashes its wrath upon you. Pine Valley, in all its unyielding, merciless splendor, is such a place. You do not whistle giddily as you stroll Pine Valley's fairways, you shudder, terrorized by your latest misfortune or the one you fear is about to manifest itself. Pine Valley exudes the school of penal architecture, where any shot less than dialled in on its target is brutalized to varying degrees. It is penal largely because it is very much a target game, where the targets on every hole get smaller and more difficult the closer you get to the cup. But the course goes about its business with a genial rhythm. It is certainly not overly long by modern standards, and even some of its longer par 4s do provide room for the run-up shot.

Its founder, George Crump, consulted with a number of famous architects of his day, and even talked extensively with H.S. Colt, who provided a routing. But this is largely Crump's package, with an able assist from Merion's designer, Hugh Wilson, who completed the four holes unfinished at the time of Crump's death. Together, Pine Valley's holes make for an exquisite symphony of promise, possibility and pain, what Robert Trent Jones Sr. once suggested constituted "more classic holes than any other course in the world."

Pine Valley is as exacting as it is exacerbating, right from the opening gun. The usually benign first hole can turn suddenly cruel if the approach is slightly long, left or right. The green at the otherwise approachable second is at least as frightening as it is elevated. Finally, the third is the kind of par 3 that can produce double digits on the scorecard; a hole perfectly in character for all of the one-shot holes here. Appropriately, each requires a significantly different club from the others, ranging from a short iron at the mercurial 10th to a stout 3-wood at the gargantuan fifth.

Crump once suggested that the difficulties at Pine Valley only discouraged "the dub golfers," that Pine Valley "is a course for champions, and they never get into trouble."

But they have to get into trouble at Pine Valley because, simply, it is everywhere. Every hole is edged with trees, scrub or sandy waste areas that sometimes can be even more penalizing than water hazards or out-of-bounds. Elsewhere, there are maniacally contoured greens and hazards that have lives of their own. Such is the 90-yard-long and fairway-wide bunker at the seventh, known as "Hell's Half-Acre." Even a microscopically off-line tee ball means the huge waste area can't be carried with the second shot, and that quickly means the 585-yard par 5 turns into a par 7.

The back nine's intensity builds measurably, starting with the heroic 448-yard 13th hole where the bold second shot

challenges a deep, sandy waste area guarding the hole's entire left side. The epic 15th is a fully outfitted hike of a par 5 where a 14 has been recorded by a competitor in the prestigious annual Crump Cup amateur tournament. The final three holes are as strong an ending to the day as the first three are a beginning: the slightly uphill approach over a valley to the huge, heavily bunkered 18th green providing one last unrelenting examination in the marathon.

Jay Sigel, the decorated amateur and eventual Senior Tour standout, has conquered Pine Valley on several occasions, winning the Crump Cup nine times and serving as player-captain to the victorious U.S. side in the 1985 Walker Cup. He speaks for all of Pine Valley's fans and victims when he says, "You love it, and you hate it. It's beautiful, and it's horrible. It's wonderful, and yet it's just so darn difficult."

1936: Led by non-playing captain Francis Ouimet, the U.S. records the only shutout in the history of the Walker Cup before or since, defeating the team from Great Britain and Ireland, 9–0.

1961: Gene Littler and Byron Nelson square off in a Shell's Wonderful World of Golf match, and Littler, the reigning U.S. Open champion, only manages a 78 and Nelson cruises to victory with a hard-fought 74.

1985: Career amateur Bob Lewis, who once set the course record with a 64, clinches the deciding point for a U.S. squad that includes Davis Love III, as it defeats Great Britain and Ireland 13–11 in the Walker Cup.

DEFINING MOMENTS

1960: Jack Nicklaus, in the middle of his honeymoon, plays as an invited guest. Because the club rules bar women, his wife Barbara is driven around the perimeter so she can catch a glimpse of him through the trees.

The midsection of the long 7th hole is desecrated by 'Hell's half acre.'

Feature Hole

10

On this big, bad, golf course, the tenth hole seems almost innocuous. In truth, it can easily be Pine Valley's most diabolical, all because of a little pit of sand named for the Devil's least flattering orifice—and has reportedly made grown men cry. The D.A. bunker at Pine Valley's tenth hole is a most foul place, but it is so perfectly positioned that, architecturally, it is almost high art. The green actually seems substantial enough on a short hole that plays from a plateau of a tee above a field of sand and waste to a pushed-up green that seems to list in the midst of a sea of sand. But the pot bunker, a straitjacket in sand, always figures in your attack of the hole, always seems to gather a less-than-fully-hit iron or forces an extra tug on the downswing that results in just as penalizing a miss to the left or right or long. It also receives more than the occasional putt that runs off the green and into the D.A.'s den.

145 YARDS PAR 3

Prairie Dunes Country Club

| Location: **Hutchinson, Kansas** |
| Opened: **1937** |
| Architect: **Perry Maxwell/Press Maxwell (1957)** |
| Par: **70** |
| Length: **6,598 yards** |

P rairie Dunes is a fantasy located in a parallel universe disguised as a dream. It has to be. How else could you explain finding Scotland's most perfect linksland smack-dab in the middle of America's Great Plains? How it happened to be is in large part the measure of the architectural mind of Perry Maxwell. After reviewing the land proposed for Prairie Dunes, Maxwell was overwhelmed. He said then: "There are 118 golf holes here. All I have to do is eliminate 100." Without question the right 18 were found.

The dunes-like land is a wondrous freak of nature, the kind of land, noted golf historian Robert Somers once suggested "has a character that only a golf course architect might love." Formed aeons ago by the encroaching arctic ice shelf moving its way south, the leftovers make a unique landscape that defies the typical image of the desolate, plainsland of south central Kansas. It was once a great salt sea, but the unkempt bottomland of this long-ago ocean was born to be a golf course. Maxwell knew it, and knew enough to get out of its way. Gently he guided the land into the course's first nine golf holes, just as his son Press would do 20 years later for the remaining nine. The minute he rode into Hutchinson on the train, Maxwell knew he'd found a special place. "The area would be a wonderful site for a Scottish-type course in the valleys of those sand hills," he said.

And that's precisely what was produced. Holes move in a maddening topography, with doglegs where the preferred play is often based on faith, like at the psychotically flowing ninth, the bounding sixth and 17th holes, the debilitating 12th, where a cottonwood tree stands as bouncer, and the adventurous 14th with its monstrous left-hand bunker. Not only does the roll of the land change schizophrenically, so too does its direction. More than two-thirds of the holes have some element of bend to them, with the corner of many doglegs guarded by grassy or sandy deaths.

The first of Praire Dunes' collection of uphill par–3s is the tiny 2nd.

But as intriguing as Prairie Dunes is within the boundaries of its fairways, it's what lies outside the preferred line of play that grabs even the most resolute ball striker by the scruff of the neck and plagues him with uncertainty. The rough areas include neck high fields of bluestem, yucca plants and wild plum thickets, plus sunflowers, cottonwoods, crowfoot grass and milkweed. Wildflowers like asters, thistles, black-eyed Susans and cockleburs lend color to an already unruly tableau. In some places the wild forests of yucca plants grow right up in the middle of bunkers, too, just for sport. Says honorary member Tom Watson, "The basic concept of the course is some fairway, a little bit of rough and a whole lot of heavy junk that's like Scottish heather and gorse. It's enjoyable to play, but very difficult when the wind gets up, even for the best players." Members

often play the wild thick grass separating fairways as lateral hazards, and not just because they don't think they'll find their ball. It seems the high grass is home to bullsnakes, too.

Of course, there is one other factor at Prairie Dunes that brings to mind true Scottish linksland: the omnipresent breeze. Some locals say a normal wind at Prairie Dunes is 25 miles per hour, so it's certain the layout plays bigger than the 6,598 yards listed on the scorecard.

It has been called the Pine Valley of the West, but that reference places a limitation on the character of Prairie Dunes. It is a thoroughly original place, unmatched certainly in America, if not the entire golfing world. As was said by Judy Bell, who captained an American Curtis Cup team here in 1986, "You'd have to go to heaven to play on a course this fine. It's pure. It tests all you've got in your game."

Feature Hole

There are many who regard this bounding dogleg right as the best eighth hole in the country. Others say the same, leaving off the word "eighth." No. 8 is a walk on the moon with its rumpled, rumbling fairway combined with a triple-tiered green. It is a hole full of overwhelming movement and portent. Prairie Dunes' characteristic wild rough lies at the corner of the dogleg here, discouraging the overly bold. But even the middle of the fairway has its obstacles, a series of four heaving swales and dune hiccups that reach 40 feet high. Even a well struck tee ball is no reward, though, because the player is left with an unlevel lie to the raucous green, with five bunkers clearly in play and an absolute nightmare of tall grass and despair laying in wait beyond the putting surface. No wonder during the 1986 Curtis Cup the stroke average was an alarming 4.75.

430 YARDS

PAR 4

Menacing vegetation is everywhere at Prarie Dunes, especially at the closing hole.

1958: Never managing to shoot a round under 72, Jack Nicklaus wins the Trans-Mississippi Amateur. It begins a string of seven straight rounds Nicklaus plays on the course without breaking par.

1962: Arnold Palmer and Jack Nicklaus play an exhibition at Prairie Dunes in 100-degree heat and heavy rough that exacts a toll. Palmer shoots 72, Nicklaus, who visits the rough on ten different holes, shoots 77.

1980: Juli Inkster, a 21-year-old newlywed, wins the first of three U.S. Women's Amateur titles, winning the 18-hole final over Patti Rizzo two up.

2002: Juli Inkster rallies with a stirring final round 66 to overtake top-ranked Annika Sorenstam and win her second U.S. Women's Open crown.

DEFINING MOMENTS

1964: Barbara McIntire defeats Joanne Gunderson in the U.S. Women's Amateur. Earlier in the week Gunderson shot 70 to set the women's course record.

1986: The Great Britain and Ireland squad, which had lost the 13 previous Curtis Cup matches and had never before won in the U.S., defeats an American team that features four future LPGA tour professionals, 13–5.

The perched green makes the Center's signature 6th hole perilous.

Ridgewood Country Club

Location: **Paramus, New Jersey**
Opened: **1929**
Architect: **A.W. Tillinghast**
Par: **35 (East); 36 (West); 36 (Center)**
Length: **3,411 yds (E); 3,534 yds (W); 3,345 yds (C)**

New Jersey's staid Ridgewood Country Club may not be the best 18 holes in one place—the candidates for that honor are well-qualified and numerous—but it may stand alone as a collection of 27 holes. It certainly did for its creator, the inimitable A.W. Tillinghast.

Though he had already produced prodigious 36-hole masterpieces at Baltusrol and Winged Foot before he set up shop in a personally selected plot of ground in the New Jersey outskirts of New York City—those two would get more attention as they played host to one U.S. Golf Association championship after another over the years— Ridgewood is routinely mentioned as Tillinghast's favorite. He even maintained a membership there after he moved west to California in his later days.

When he completed his work at Ridgewood, he left behind 27 holes of unwavering intensity and a challenge of beauty and simplicity. Their strength individually can best be detailed by this one fact: For the handful of significant golf events that have been played at Ridgewood over the decades (a U.S. Amateur, a U.S. Senior Open, a Senior PGA Championship, among others) all 27 holes have been used at one time or another. It is all due to the magical perspective of Tillinghast, who not only did the design but supervised the construction on a daily basis and even set about improving it time and again over the next several years. At every tee, Ridgewood defines one of Tillinghast's overriding tenets: "A round of golf should present 18 inspirations." At Ridgewood, there are 27.

It is a game of change and challenge at Ridgewood. Just when you've settled into a rhythm, the tune takes a new beat. Your first two approaches to greens on the Center course are with similar clubs, but the first is to an open green, then to one completely blocked in front. On the West course, you can bounce the ball into the first three greens and then must fly it in to the next three. And while the majority of the holes at Ridgewood call for a draw off the tee, the championship usually ends on the final hole of the West 9, which, of course, asks the player to hit a fade.

Since Ridgewood plays through corridors of hardwoods that have grown up and out over the years, driving accurately is even more of a requirement than it might have been in Tillinghast's day. Tillinghast wasn't especially fond of having the joy of playing a hole ruined by the first swing. Still, it is not a course that lets a player bomb it without restraint. Indeed, well hit tee balls that fly straight more than occasionally run out of fairway.

The look of the second shots vary in confounding ways, whether it be the flowing or sculpted bunkers seen at holes like the West second and the Center second and seventh, the deceptive traps 10 and 20 yards short of several greens like on the West 5th, or the pushed up tiny greens like at Center No. 4. Even green complexes confound approach shots, like at the East's par-3 sixth, a 229-yard downhiller with a green that slopes from front to back.

Tillinghast further mixes things up with a hole like the 289-yard sixth on the Center, where a sliver of a green decorated with five bunkers can make even the best players look silly. Jack Nicklaus missed the green from the fairway four days in a row at the 1990 U.S. Senior Open.

The ultimate joy of Ridgewood is that unlike Winged Foot and Baltusrol, there is never a hint of sameness. Said Rees Jones, "He is trying to make sure that when you finish you will think you have played 18 distinctly different holes. That's why he's my architectural hero."

1935: Ridgewood member James Black helps save the Ryder Cup when he suggests the matches switch from June to September. The British, disgruntled with the heat of June, and on the verge of quitting, agree, but still lose 9–3.

1990: Arnold Palmer, Jack Nicklaus, Gary Player and Lee Trevino got together for a competitive reunion at the U.S. Senior Open. Nicklaus had the third-round lead, but Merry Mex's final round 67 gave him the victory.

2001: Tom Watson and Jim Thorpe duel down to the 72nd hole at the Senior PGA Championship. Watson prevails by one as Thorpe misses a seven-foot birdie putt at the 72nd hole.

DEFINING MOMENTS

1974: Jerry Pate, a 20-year-old student at the University of Alabama, wins the U.S. Amateur, defeating John Grace 2&1 in the final. Pate beats Bill Campbell and Curtis Strange along the way.

The green at the Center's par–4 7th is tucked to the right of artful bunkers.

Feature Hole

8 (WEST)

A monumentally strong hole at a perfect moment in the round (it has played as the 17th in major events), this is one of the great par 5s in golf. It is a beautiful collection of teases and temptations, especially interesting for a three-shot hole. As Rees Jones said, "Tillinghast designed it so that if you don't at least flirt with the tree line left, you risk hitting through the fairway on the right." At minimum, a tulip tree encroaching on the right side of the fairway blocks the angle for second-shot attempts from the right edge of the fairway. Tillinghast provides this challenge off the tee without a fairway bunker. Then, knowing that the third shot would be made with one of the more precise clubs in the bag, he finished the fun with a miniscule green guarded on the left by the deepest bunker on the property.

569 YARDS

PAR 5

Riviera Country Club

Location: **Pacific Palisades, California**
Opened: **1926**
Architect: **George C. Thomas Jr./William P. Bell**
Par: **72**
Length: **7,256 yards**

Built in the shadow of Hollywood and poised to be the club of choice for the film world's stars and moguls, Riviera Country Club was a big budget picture in the making. Indeed, it cost easily three times as much to build the golf course as the going rate for golf course construction in the 1920s and used the most extensive collection of motorized equipment ever assembled for a golf course project. But just like *Gone With the Wind*, Riviera was a blockbuster smash hit from its first viewing. Not, however, because of the stars or the big names, not because it became a favorite of the game's greats like Hogan, Snead and Nelson and not even because of its setting in the Santa Monica canyon. Riviera's critical acclaim arose not from its big budget, scenic locale or glamorous clientele, but from the calculated style of a man who designed the course for free.

George Thomas, an amateur architect who was independently wealthy, had gained notoriety for successful designs at Bel-Air and Los Angeles Country Club's North Course, where he also worked for free, but, in Riviera, he and his right-hand man, Billy Bell, knew they might be unearthing a pure, strategic golf design gem.

As Thomas mentioned in a local paper prior to the opening, the course "will be majestic, a thing of colossal beauty and still a golf course which will afford the maximum of pleasure to young and old, strong and weak."

Today, Riviera remains just that sort of pleasing test. Smallish greens are guarded by inscrutable bunkers that at times seem almost lyrical in design. Fairways and greens are bordered by eucalyptus and sycamore trees and a perplexing brillo-like rough of kikuyu grass that occasionally leaves a player wishing he had dyanmite to go with his sand wedge.

Riviera does not need a brass band announcing its arrival or welcoming its return. It sounds the call on its own. On the opening par 5, the near 100-foot drop from first tee to

The drivable par–4 10th provides the perfect example of the clever bunkering that is one of Riviera's hallmarks.

first fairway is sufficiently grand to let you know you have arrived somewhere special. And its finishing hole is one of golf's all-time greats. But throughout the course, the tests come in all forms. The player is treated to a variety of par 4s, some driveable, some occasionally requiring two full woods to reach the putting surface. While Ben Hogan suggested the 236-yard fourth hole was the best par 3 in the world, it is the sixth that stands out in most people's minds, largely because there is a circular pit of sand right in the middle of the green.

Its longer holes like Nos. 2, 9, 15 and, of course, 18 are the supreme driving tests that appealed to Hogan, who won here three times in a 17-month span (two L.A. Opens and the U.S. Open in 1948). But Riviera's special delight comes in a short par 4, like the driveable 10th, where bunkers linger in every corner and figure in every decision. Thomas'

bunkering is stirring stuff and their strategic placement is legendary. Shortly after Riviera opened, Thomas' book *Golf Architecture in America* was published. In it, he explained strategic design this way: "There must be enough risk to lend zest to play, without undue punishment; and if natural dangers are not present, artificial ones should be constructed. The course which demands the greatest number of placements from the tee and the most diversity of shots is the best test."

Thomas provided such a test at Riviera, his final design and a fitting memorial. As honorary member Ben Crenshaw once wrote in the club's official history, "Riviera serves as a supreme test for every golfer…The golfer is confronted with 18 separate problems which require that extremely rare balance of mental and physical, or skilled effort."

Feature Hole

Pulitzer Prize-winning sports columnist Jim Murray once referred to Riviera's epic 18th hole as "the plu-perfect finishing hole in the game of golf…451 yards of heartbreak." It is the sort of finishing hole you want for a championship. While the hole doglegs right along a line of eucalyptus trees that grew up with the course, thick kikuyu rough and a hillside on the left keep the safe side of the fairway honest. As players climb the hill to their drives, Riviera's stately clubhouse comes into view, temporarily distracting them from their difficult approach shots. Despite Thomas' gifts in bunker design, there is no sand closely guarding the 18th green. Just a green that slopes wickedly away from the hillside. Says Jack Nicklaus, "It is a very strong hole, a great finishing hole, and one of my favorite holes."

451 YARDS

PAR 4

The 6th hole is Riviera's most unique offering, featuring a bunker situated in the middle of its green

1929: The Los Angeles City Junior Chamber of Commerce, hoping to find a course that would be "a real test for the Hagens, Farrells and Espinozas," moves the Los Angeles Open to Riviera Country Club.

1945: Sam Snead wins the L.A. Open at Riviera, starting a string where he, Byron Nelson, Ben Hogan or Lloyd Mangrum would combine to win eight of the next nine L.A. Opens at Riviera.

1983: A 25-year-old Hal Sutton holds off a charging Jack Nicklaus to win the PGA Championship, making a crucial closing par on the final hole to win by one.

DEFINING MOMENTS

1948: Riviera was christened "Hogan's Alley," as Hogan sets a new tournament record of 276 in the U.S. Open. It is Hogan's third victory in 17 months at the course, including L.A. Open titles in both 1947 and '48.

1998: Hale Irwin birdies two of the final three holes, including the epic 18th, to win his first U.S. Senior Open title.

The 2nd hole features an uphill climb and a bunker well short of the green that distorts perception.

Salem Country Club

Location: **Peabody, Massachusetts**
Opened: **1926**
Architect: **Donald Ross**
Par: **72**
Length: **6,823 yards**

It took barely 50 words for Donald Ross to explain what he called his "design standards." Detailed in his memoirs, *Golf Has Never Failed Me*, they read: "Make each hole present a different problem. So arrange it that every stroke must be made with a full concentration and attention necessary to good golf. Build each hole in such a manner that it wastes none of the ground at my disposal, and takes advantage of every possibility I can see."

Of course, he could have said it even more economically. He could have simply said, "See Salem Country Club."

Clearly, Ross was in full flight at Salem, and even to this day, Salem remains largely as Ross first proposed it. Its challenge, too, has remained consistent throughout the years. Winning scores at the three major events played there have varied microscopically, from three-over at the 1954 U.S. Women's Open to two-over at the 1984 U.S. Women's to even-par at the 2001 U.S. Senior Open.

The land Ross saw for the course at Salem was rugged and forested. Reports from the club history indicate that a crew of 300 men and 40 teams of horses did the work at Salem (notice there were no bulldozers). The clearing of the land resulted in 1,000 cords of wood being cut down and blasting through the rocky land required ten tons of dynamite.

But Ross' design fits the land. Holes bend right as many times as they bend left, and there are as many holes under 400 yards long as there are over 400 yards. Uphill mixes with downhill and natural ridge lines and breaks are incorporated into the layout rather than circumvented. Unlike what was the norm in Ross' day, the bunkers are merely an ingredient here (there are just 54 on the entire course, about half the amount of another of Ross' courses, Scioto); they do not dominate the experience, only enhance it, directing the action and keeping the bold player honest.

The greens are wonderfully natural and naturally tricky,

although Jack Nicklaus once suggested that if he were to build such greens, "the owner wouldn't pay me and he'd sue me." In truth, Salem's greens epitomize one of Ross' architectural edicts, "Select your putting green locations if possible to give desirable, undulating surfaces. Nature does this sort of thing best." But Ross' greens were well-planned and their slopes vary in direction, dismissing the idea that all greens need to slope to the front. Indeed, the whole course makes good use of the land. Fairways bound along with hardly a flat lie to be found.

Fittingly, Ross starts the day trying to breed confidence with an elevated tee shot and a bunkerless green, but it isn't a listless start because a poor tee ball brings flanking bunkers well short of the green into play. The short cross hazard comes into play elsewhere, like at the ninth, where a pond

40 yards short of the green means anything less than an accurate drive will force the player to be especially brave or especially conservative on his second shot. And the par 3s are demanding, as Ross believed they should be, since every player starts these holes with a perfect lie. No. 12 is especially exemplary because while it is the shortest hole on the course, it is also the most heavily bunkered.

In true Ross fashion, Salem's challenge remains measured: it demands more from the accomplished player than from the novice. Even Nicklaus admired that, saying, "I think for normal member play, it's a very fun, roaming golf course...but when it gets firm, it's a golf course where it's difficult to manage your game. The ball can be bouncing in all kinds of directions, and you've just got to be aware of it. If you are, you can shoot a good score."

1932: In a clash of the titans of women's amateur golf in America, Virginia Van Wie upends Glenna Collett Vare in the final of the U.S. Women's Amateur to win the first of her three national titles in a row.

1954: Babe Didrikson Zaharias, 15 months after colon cancer surgery, destroyed the field at the U.S. Women's Open, finishing at three-over par and winning by a still-record 12 shots. Zaharias died just two years later.

2001: Bruce Fleisher wins his first U.S. Senior Open, finishing at even par. He joined Jack Nicklaus as the only men to win both a U.S. Amateur title and a U.S. Senior Open.

DEFINING **MOMENTS**

1984: Hollis Stacy finishes with a two-over par total of 290 to win her third U.S. Women's Open in a span of seven years. She defeats Rosie Jones by a single shot with a final round 69, the low round of the tournament.

Feature Hole

13

A treacherously framed, sharply angled dogleg forces players to play to the left side of the snaking fairway, but with the landing area sloping left to right, getting the ball in an ideal position off the tee requires a certain level of discretion. The deep, grass-faced bunker on the right is probably not in play, but it gets the player aiming well left off the tee, which provides the best line in, until he goes too far left. The green is elevated, but the lie in the rumpled bedspread of a fairway can often be trickily downhill. That, of course, encourages a miss short and right, where there's a steep slope and an unforgiving bunker. The green has a ridge running through it and seems to slope in every direction. In fact, so particular was Ross about the construction of the putting surface that he eventually referred to it as "the finest green I ever designed."

342 YARDS

PAR 4

It's hard to choose which bunker is less appetizing, the one well in front of the 16th green or the one sunk in to its right side.

Sand Hills Golf Club

Location: **Mullen, Nebraska**
Opened: **1994**
Architect: **Bill Coore and Ben Crenshaw**
Par: **71**
Length: **7,089 yards**

Some will argue that Sand Hills Golf Club, hidden in the rumples and folds of northwest Nebraska's barren landscape, makes no sense. It is, after all, an hour or more from the nearest real city, five hours from the nearest sizeable airport. It is, one would think, a hell of a strange place to build a golf course, let alone one that would become elevated to the status of a near religious retreat. But just as quickly, someone else (most likely someone who has been to these wildly wide-open lands of quiet power to see and soak up Sand Hills) is likely to argue another point, namely, that visionary architects Bill Coore and Ben Crenshaw didn't really build a golf course here. Instead, they found one.

No, Sand Hills doesn't make any sense. How is it, for instance, that America's perfect true linksland actually lies thousands of miles in either direction from any ocean? But that is surely what the topography of Sand Hills suggests. This is links golf, raw and windblown, bouncy and unpredictable, inventive and changing, abruptly rugged and infinitesimally subtle. How ideal was the setting that would become the 18 holes at Sand Hills?

So enraptured were Coore and Crenshaw that they saw nearly eight full golf courses worth of holes on the property before settling on the final 18-hole layout. How much was the course already there? Consider that the grading for the entire course took not much more than a morning's work. "It's discovery, not creation," Crenshaw said at the time. "All we do is scrape off the existing vegetation and seed."

When the golfer thinks of pilgrimages, it is normally to places offering a sampler of golf courses. Yet the solitary 18 at Sand Hills seems more than enough, satisfying in different ways on different days. Here, the wind, unobstructed, comes at the player from every conceivable angle. If golf's full examination comes only when a wind blows, then there is little doubt that the test at Sand Hills is the ultimate.

The undulating fairway of the 9th seems enough to induce motion sickness.

But even if Sand Hills makes no sense being here, it is clear that what was found in this place was a golf course that not merely finds steady, comfortable and natural purchase in the land, but one that is a natural manifestation of golf's more spiritual side. The dunes and natural blowout bunkers were already here waiting to have greens and fairways routed around them. The unadorned holes (there are no water hazards) are refreshingly unlike any others in the world, yet viewed for the first time, they appear fundamentally and instinctively reflective of golf's soul.

It is not fair to pick them out from among their brethren, because it is like removing threads from a tapestry. Still, if only to provide a glimmer of the possibility of the perfection of Sand Hills, there must be mention of these. There's the incomparable opener, a par 5 from an elevated tee that seems to present all of the universe in the distance. There are the quirky, but fantastic, shorter par 4s, like the fifth with its bunker spotted right in the center of the fairway and the seventh, which begs to be driven, but should not be. The back nine can play some 300 yards longer than the front, with stouter par 4s but a healthy measure of precision, too. Its final three holes, including the serpentine 16th and the ticklish 17th, are a stupendous mix and finish with a big drive over a deep dune followed by a big iron over an even deeper bunker by the green.

These are the kind of holes when combined as one make for the sort of memories that linger well after this quiet place has been left behind for the real world. Like the entire essence of this place, they are challenging, they are varied and they are unsurpassed.

Feature Hole

17

The perfection of Sand Hills manifests itself in so many unexpected ways. One that might be expected, however, is the routing. The almost symphonic juxtaposition of challenges at Sand Hills is revealed most dramatically at the end, and especially at the penultimate hole. Here, the downhill par 3 to a blowout-shrouded fig leaf of a green lies in perfect contrast to the brutish par 5 that precedes it and the herculean par-4 finisher. Sitting atop a ridge, the 17th is victim to the constant breeze and the occasional 40 mile-per-hour gusts. A windmill lurks behind the green, eerie yet soothing at the same time. The shot to the green is all finesse, like a free throw late in the game after you've run full court. Says Crenshaw: "This was a hole we thought would be ideal coming after a par 5 that is more of a power and placement hole. It requires a delicate stroke."

150 YARDS

PAR 3

The second of consecutive shortish par–4s, the eighth is protected by a bunker that gouges the front of the green.

1992: The design team of Bill Coore and Ben Crenshaw are asked by Sand Hills developer Dick Youngscap to survey possible sites. Said Coore: "It was incredible. We weren't prepared for what we saw."

1999: Sand Hills debuts at No. 31 on *Golf Digest*'s ranking of America's 100 Greatest Courses. It is the highest postion for a course making its debut on the list that year.

DEFINING **MOMENTS**

1993: In all Coore and Crenshaw lay out 136 different holes to fit in the property, eventually settling on a final 18. Grading of the course cost a grand total of $7,500.

1995: Sand Hills is named the Best New Course in America by *Golf Digest*.

San Francisco Golf Club

Location: **San Francisco, California**
Opened: **1918**
Architect: **A. W. Tillinghast**
Par: **71**
Length: **6,716 yards**

San Francisco Golf Club is a quiet place that much of the world is waiting to discover, and most likely never will. This is, of course, how the members prefer it. There are more famous courses by A.W. Tillinghast (Winged Foot, for one, Baltusrol, for another). There are more recognized courses even within the city limits (like the nearby Olympic Club), but San Francisco Golf Club has never been about the fame or the recognition. Here, the requirements are simpler, yet more fulfilling. It is a good walk. With friends. With 18 holes that challenge gently, but in full.

The thing that eventually overwhelms you about the place is just how complete it is. It lacks nothing, or at least nothing that matters. It was not unusual in years past for groups of five, six or even seven players to troop off together for a round or an extra nine holes in the quiet of the evening. Maybe this sense is derived from the character of the club itself, which is decidedly unadorned and resoundingly uncompromising, but no less a contributor to that prevailing mood is its golf course.

San Francisco Golf Club might very well be as riveting an example of the best golf architecture the Golden Age had to offer. It clearly stands as grand evidence of the versatility of A.W. Tillinghast. Frank Hannigan, former senior executive director of the U.S. Golf Association once wrote: "Tillinghast's greatest assets were his rich intelligence, imagination and sense of aesthetics. He did not repeat himself; his best courses are marked by variety…"

Variety is precisely what can be found at San Francisco Golf Club. While the land moves in many directions here, Tillinghast's holes fit their surroundings effortlessly. While the beautiful par-3 seventh has long been lauded as one of Tillinghast's favorite holes, it is just one example of the tempered feel to the proceedings here. Harvie Ward, the legendary amateur who won back-to-back U.S. national titles

Trees play a restrained but purposeful role at San Francisco Golf Club, like at the 10th hole

in 1955 and 1956, once remarked, "San Francisco is such a neat course. You don't ever get tired of playing it."

Even today, after the holes have been lengthened, it is still as comfortable as a favorite sweater. The opener is a sometimes reachable, sometimes not, par 5, where the wind is the deciding factor. Indeed, the conditions here can make the course feel and play much longer than its yardage. (But just as quickly the weather can change and play gets firm and fast. The characteristics of the challenge may change, but the intensity does not.) Atypically, just one bunker waits by the first green. It is a scene not repeated often through the rest of the day. Instead, Tillinghast's much preferred "well guarded green" is the standard treatment here, most notably at mid-length par-4 holes like the eighth and 16th.

This is a course of consummate sand hazards, sculpted

from the terrain as if by an artisan and vastly different than the monstrous traps in Tillinghast's work at Bethpage Black. Beautiful to view, they still can be completely disarming. While the bunkers border on the intimidating on many of the par 3s and on holes like the uphill par-5 ninth (with nine) and the equally arduous 18th (with eleven), they seem almost good fun on holes like the tenth, where they encourage and reward a bold line.

San Francisco Golf Club may be a simple, quiet place on golf's stage, but it satisfies all Tillinghast ever asked of one of his designs. He once wrote: "In the planning of courses, there is the joy of creation, and a keen satisfaction in seeing them develop, until finally they receive the approval of those who play over them." All those who play over San Francisco Golf Club surely approve.

1918: The San Francisco Golf Club opens at its third site, moving first from a nine-hole course at The Presidio opened in 1895 and then the second site at Ingleside in 1905, from which it had to move after losing its lease.

1938: Jimmy Demaret defeats Sam Snead in the San Francisco Matchplay Championship, the only individual tournament ever conducted at San Francisco Golf Club.

1974: In typically foggy, chilly conditions, the U.S. defeats Great Britain and Ireland in the Curtis Cup, 13–5. Jane Bastanchury Booth (below) leads the U.S. side with two singles wins and two foursomes wins.

DEFINING **MOMENTS**

1927: A report in a golf publication highlights the San Francisco Golf Club, "which whispers say is to be the scene of the 1929 National Amateur." Instead, the U.S. Amateur is held to the south at Pebble Beach.

The staunch second swings downhill then uphill to a well-guarded green,

Feature Hole

7

A.W. Tillinghast, the man who also designed the infamous par-3 10th hole at Winged Foot's West course, reportedly called this hole one of his favorites of all time. It is attention-grabbing for several reasons. First, the tee shot plays well downhill to a green protected by bunkers and a natural fall-off to the right. The green itself has enough roll to force players to not merely land anywhere on the putting surface, but in the right section of the green. Aside from its deceptively cozy feel, the hole's real charm is its place in history. The last formal duel in the U.S. took place at a spot just to the right of the green nearly 60 years before Tillinghast built the golf course. Two small granite obelisks mark the historic occasion where state Supreme Court Justice David Terry mortally wounded U.S. Senator David Broderick in September 1859. The two men apparently disagreed over the preservation of the Union.

190 YARDS

PAR 3

Scioto
Country Club

Location: **Columbus, Ohio**
Opened: **1916**
Architect: **Donald Ross**
Par: **71**
Length: **6,950 yards**

No one even marginally informed about golf would say, that without Scioto Country Club Jack Nicklaus would not have developed into the greatest golfer in the history of the game. But it didn't hurt.

Nicklaus started playing golf at age 10 at Scioto as he tagged along with his father Charlie in round after round. It was at Scioto that Nicklaus fell under the expert tutelage of golf instructor Jack Grout, the man who would develop the young Nicklaus swing and who would routinely hone Nicklaus' development into a complete champion. But it may have been the overall challenge and intrigue of Scioto's design that fostered in Nicklaus an appreciation for the special mental and physical skill set that only golf on a truly great course can demand. "Scioto, when I was growing up, was a wonderful course," Nicklaus has said.

Donald Ross designed the Scioto that Nicklaus' game developed on, and while the changes installed during Dick Wilson's redesign in the 1960s have irked some Ross fans, the overriding themes and rhythms of the course have not been erased. Scioto is still a course of great approach shots, even though driving is of a premium as trees lining the fairways have grown up in the course's first eight decades. Though it is hardly a drive-and-flick experience, it is still a course where the value of the tee shot occasionally places positioning over power. In addition, every green is blocked or flanked by bunkers, and while Ross provides openings in front of most holes, getting the ball close to the most trying hole locations requires both finesse and fearlessness.

On the first four holes Scioto mixes brute force with tactics, a perfect primer for the remainder of the day's challenge. For instance, the first and third holes are shortish par 4s, while the infamous second, and the long par-3 fourth, demand near perfection. The second is seen as one of the game's great holes, an uphill mammoth par 4 with a hidden

The short 17th has been lengthened and bolstered by a pond over the years.

stream in play on the left side and out-of-bounds on the right. A tee shot that does not reach the crown of the fairway leaves the player with no sight of the green, which is elevated enough to thwart a run-up shot.

Ross never dictates only one type of play, however, and Scioto is a shining example of that. Holes bend in both directions an equal number of times off the tee. Longer par 4s are open in front, while those requiring short-iron second shots, like the 378-yard seventh and the 360-yard 11th, tend to be protected by sand. And even the par-3 ninth, now the shortest hole on the course, was so confounding that Bobby Jones was unable to par it in four rounds during the 1926 U.S. Open, which he won.

Even the long holes at Scioto are a mental test, too. Like the par-5 12th, the longest hole on the course, a dip in the fairway at the landing area means the second shot can be partially blind, or the long par-4 16th, where trees cutting in from the left suggest that a tee shot on the dogleg right would be best positioned on the right side of the fairway.

Everywhere Scioto is exacting, and in the back of your mind, you can see the calculating persona of a Nicklaus beginning to warm to the challenge of the game as it had to be played on his home course. "The biggest influence on my game from my early years at Scioto," said Nicklaus, "was the fact that all of the out-of-bounds at Scioto were on the right. From the beginning, I always played to the center of the fairway with a fade." That controlled fade would go on to serve Nickaus well, given his record of 18 professional major championships. So would the education he got playing such a test as Scioto every day.

Feature Hole

8

Though this hole was played as a par 4 during the 1968 U.S. Amateur, its real character is as a classic risk-reward par 5. Its look remains one of golf's most distinctive, and Dick Wilson's changes, which included an additional fairway bunker and slightly elevating the green to help in drainage issues, make it play even stronger. A long, aggressive second shot must carry first the Scioto River and a lake that guards the front left half of the green and then must land on a green that is itself surrounded by almost a moat of a water hazard. The real sport of Scioto's eighth is how the challenge to go at the green in two is only slightly greater than the twin tests of a successful layup shot and short third. Compounding the difficulty is the narrow fairway, menaced by the water on the left and trees on the right. And still the player must negotiate a third shot that has water and bunkers in play to torment anything but a confident swing.

509 YARDS

PAR 5

The long, angling par–4 16th tests tee ball, approach shot, and fortitude.

1926: Defeating Joe Turnesa by a single shot after a birdie on the last hole, Bobby Jones wins the second of his four U.S. Open titles, becoming the first man ever to hold both the U.S. Open and the British Open in the same year.

1931: A U.S. squad, featuring the likes of Gene Sarazen, Walter Hagen and Denny Shute subdue the British side 9–3 in the third Ryder Cup matches. Of the 12 matches, the U.S. wins five by scores of 7&6 or better.

1950: In an unexpected, and as many would say, unwanted final for the PGA Championship, Chandler Harper defeats Henry Williams 4&3. Harper (below) plays his first four matches in a combined 20-under par.

DEFINING MOMENTS

1953: Jack Nicklaus, playing with his father and breaking up his front and back nines to run home and eat dinner, shoots under 70 for the first time at the age of 13, making an eagle on the final hole.

Seminole Golf Club

Location: **North Palm Beach, Florida**
Opened: **1929**
Architect: **Donald Ross**
Par: **72**
Length: **6,787 yards**

Donald Ross has his name on the plans for some 600 golf courses, but the story goes that the project that would eventually become Seminole Golf Club was the only one in his storied architecture career he actively pursued. Think Seminole might be any good?

Well, while others have suggested it might be his best course ever, Ross himself never said for sure. But he did hint at it. He says of Seminole simply this: "I don't say it is the best I have ever designed. Nevertheless, I like it very much."

Ross had few, if any, sites as arresting as Seminole, perched amidst a pair of dune lines and hard against the Atlantic Ocean. While it would turn out to be one of his last original 18-hole projects, Seminole reveals an arresting array of Ross' facile use of natural features and strategic design.

Moreover, Seminole is the rare course that challenges each level of player with increasing severity. Exposed to the occasionally punishing south Florida winds and constricted on many sides by bunkering that is equal parts artistry and aggravation, Seminole nevertheless does not initially assault the player. As Herbert Warren Wind has put it, "It may look mild and manageable—the fairways are wide, the rough is civilized, the undulations restrained, the greens large and candid—and because of its reasonable length the average player can sometimes salvage a par after a poorish drive. Nonetheless, the course demands golf of the first order."

Of course it does. But it does so with uncanny subtlety. Ross created just enough elevation here to show the player the trouble he has in store. Fairways move in either direction, and often simply putting the ball in the shorter grass is not enough. Your aim must be specific. In addition, he built up greens just enough so that he could surround them with heaving bunkers that almost necessarily shrink the size of the target in the player's mind's eye. Finally, even with so much sand dominating the landscape (there are 187 bunkers in

The 18th swerves toward trouble, helped by the breeze.

all), plenty of times the sand is to be challenged directly, not merely steered safely away from. At holes like the par-5 third, the par-4 sixth, the par-4 16th and the par-4 18th, a player is given the opportunity to cut a corner of a dogleg and challenge as much of the bunker as he dares. Here, though, bold thought must be accompanied by bold action.

Courage is clearly in play at the par-5 15th with its alternate fairways divided by palm trees and a string of four bunkers that are not mere affectation. Its bolder route is pinched by the sort of pond that breeds cowardice. The 495-yard dogleg right provides a long but safer route to the left of a large water hazard. The enticingly aggressive play is straight toward the green, over one tongue of the hazard to a landing zone, followed by a sharply struck second shot to the well-bunkered green, again over water. The beauty of the 15th, the beauty of Seminole, is that the player has options.

Fittingly, Seminole has a powerful sense of moment, too, especially its memorable finish along the Atlantic. At No. 17, the golfer faces a gritty 175-yard par 3 into the wind to a green swarming with bunkers. Then comes a par 4 along the beach uphill to a green full of hard work. Fortunately, one of the great locker rooms in all of golf awaits.

In simplest terms, Seminole is the definitive positioning golf course. It is not so much about golf to specific targets as it is golf with specific ball flights. It is that challenge that clearly appealed to Ben Hogan, who routinely spent a month at Seminole preparing for the start of his competitive golf season at the Masters. "I used to play Seminole for 30 straight days," he once said, "and I was just as eager to play it on the 30th morning as I was on the first."

1947: Claude Harmon Sr., head professional at Seminole during the winter months before returning to Winged Foot to run the shop there, shoots consecutive 30s on the front and back nines to set a new course record of 60.

1960: Bing Crosby, an honorary member who found himself at Seminole on more than one occasion, teams with Gardner Dickinson to finish in a first-place tie in the Latham Reed Amateur-Pro Tournament.

DEFINING MOMENTS

1992: The Coleman Invitational begins and remains a springtime fixture for the game's best mid-amateur and senior amateur players. It is named after George Coleman, a former president of the club.

Seminole is awash in sand, like at the par–3 5th hole.

Feature Hole

6

The sixth typifies the strategic precision that is Seminole's stock in trade. Eleven bunkers dominate nearly every corner of the immediate landscape, making both the target off the tee and the target for the approach seem microscopic at best. But at Seminole the test is to be aggressive even on a strategic hole like this one. Says Ben Hogan, for whom the sixth was the best par 4 in the world: "You can bite off as much of those bunkers on the left as you think you are big enough to bite off." Given the significant slope of the fairway, it even becomes difficult to keep the ball on the proper portion of the fairway. Of course, playing well right of the sand off the tee only leaves a severely difficult angle to attack the green. Complicating matters is the thin, long "crooked" green, where as many as three different irons can be used depending on the pin placement.

383 YARDS

PAR 4

Shadow Creek

Location: **North Las Vegas, Nevada**
Opened: **1989**
Architect: **Tom Fazio**
Par: **72**
Length: **7,239 yards**

At some point in the history of the world, Shadow Creek, the pleasuredome of a golf club that was the brainchild of casino magnate Steve Wynn, may stand as an example of gross overspending, of artificial grandeur. Though Wynn has sold the club, Shadow Creek remains an unmatched example of American golf course architecture at its domineering—and at the same time, enthralling—best. It is a testament to the creative force of one of the modern game's most heralded architects, who worked completely without restriction of time, money, expense or the natural world. It is at once unsettling and enticing, not unlike the city that surrounds it, but more importantly, it is deliciously dreamy golf design, the kind that makes you forget the fact that it shouldn't even be there in the first place.

In the original club history, there is a dramatic tandem of photographs of Wynn and architect Tom Fazio standing together on a plot of land. On the left is the land prior to the construction of the golf course: Everywhere all you see is flat, desolate, rocky, lifeless, scarred and overwhelmingly dullish brown earth. On the right, the two men stand again, this time on the completed golf course. The image now is one of trees, ridges, ponds, streams, waterfalls, flowering shrubs and, everywhere as far as the eye can see, blindingly brilliant green. The message is clear: the work at Shadow Creek is that of epic transformation. The vehicle is golf, and, in this case, the vehicle is a Rolls Royce.

Of course, it is so easy to get caught up in the grandiose accouterments of Shadow Creek. The expense of construction was rumored to be in the $60 million range. Some 21,000 trees were planted to frame the holes. Animals range from mute swans to rare Reeves and Chinese ring-necked pheasants. American widgeons and even a wallaby were brought in like so many showgirls. Still, Shadow Creek remains at its core a golf experience. The mixture of holes and challenges is exquisite. The elevation changes at the right moments and in the right ways. And every tee offers both the unexpected and the intense.

Everything at the 9th hole is magically perfect, especially the design.

There is a wonderful rhythm to the entire round and even within each hole. The day starts conveniently enough and then when a player feels his feet under him, Fazio increases the difficulty of the task, like at the 443-yard third hole. Here is the first genuine two-big-shots-required test, and Fazio gives the player plenty of room without a single greenside bunker. He frames this big hole not just with artificial ridge lines and trees but the surrounding mountain scape, too. The message is clear. This is a strong hole, but two solidly struck shots, even if slightly off line, will be rewarded. It reflects Wynn's stated purpose for the course, namely that, "Shadow Creek was supposed to excite one's emotions, and then test one's golf. It wasn't designed to be the hardest test in America."

That theme continues throughout Shadow Creek. There are elevated tees on most holes (much to any golfer's preference), but then many of the targets are accented with water hazards, too. There are all-or-nothing par 3s like the fifth and 17th, inviting opening holes on both nines, and, appropriately a gambling par-5 finisher, too. But even with its staggering variety, Shadow Creek's lines remain clear. The proper play is always easily deduced, breeding confidence. Maybe that's why the course record is 62.

In short, Shadow Creek is a spectacle, but an alluring, welcoming one that is hard to resist. Everything is just right, but then that is to be expected. As Wynn once wrote, "When you design a course like Shadow Creek, you can do anything you want because Mother Nature doesn't stand in your way." This much is clear about Shadow Creek (unlike any course ever constructed before): she didn't and they did.

Feature Hole

17

It is virtually impossible to select one hole at Shadow Creek as being the most supreme suspension of reality, but the 17th is clearly a step into another world. Staring from the tee of this downhill par 3, not only do you not believe you are in the barren desert, you're not sure you're even on the planet Earth. This is something from a dream world, as a choir of imported pine trees accented by a waterfall envelop a tiny green guarded by water (check out the swans!) and bunkers on all sides. All of this topography was created by Tom Fazio from the flat desert land, an effect Steve Wynn giddily called "an obvious crowd-pleaser." In club history Wynn says of the 17th, "Had we delivered this kind of treatment too often, it might have been excessive. But it was irresistible to do it once."

164 YARDS

PAR 3

At one time on the par–3 8th hole, golfers emerged from a tunnel to witness horticultural abundance.

175

1989: Tom Fazio (right) and Steve Wynn's dream course opens for business.

1995: The presidential campaign of Bob Dole gets a boost when a political fundraising event is held at Shadow Creek, raising $500,000 for Dole's cause.

DEFINING **MOMENTS**

1994: In its first year of eligibility for *Golf Digest*'s ranking of America's 100 Greatest Courses, Shadow Creek debuts at No. 8, the highest initial ranking of any course since the rankings began in 1966.

1998: Initially a private facility for members and special guests staying at his hotels, Wynn opens up Shadow Creek to all guests. But admission comes at a heavy price: green fees are $1,000, including caddie and limo service.

2000: Wynn sells his Mirage Hotel properties to MGM and included in the deal is access to Shadow Creek. The fees are reduced to $500, and Shadow Creek settles in at No. 31 on the *Golf Digest* ranking.

Ten bunkers obscure the target at the long 16th.

Shinnecock Hills Golf Club

Location: **Southampton, New York**
Opened: **1891**
Architect: **William Flynn (1931)**
Par: **70**
Length: **6,944 yards**

I f American golf has a noble side, then Shinnecock Hills Golf Club, on the eastern tip of Long Island, would be its enlightened king, perfect and powerful and proud. Shinnecock exudes the game's Scottish heritage, where the wind, deep whispy rough, firm soil and bouncy turf characterize the order of business. It was then U.S. Golf Association senior executive director Frank Hannigan who orchestrated the return of the U.S. Open to Shinnecock in 1986 after a 90-year absence. What pushed him to take the U.S. Open to a remote site that did not have the infrastructure to put on the biggest event in American golf was the purest, simplest logic: It was the golf course that sold him. Said Hannigan later, "Shinnecock is what golf would be like if it were invented today."

Not only was Shinnecock Hills among the founding five member clubs of the USGA and among the first to have an 18-hole golf course, it also was the site of the first specifically designed clubhouse. The house, set on the highest point on the property and designed memorably by Stanford White, is a serene yet distinctively majestic white-columned affair covered in wood shakes now weathered like the graying temples of a distinguished elder statesman. But just a few steps from the clubhouse lies an even more impressive site. From the first tee box much of the course spreads out below—waiting there like a grand buffet—still Peconic Bay shimmering in the distance. Here, the challenge of the entire golf course is clear from the first tee. Here, the golfer feels the power of Shinnecock's co-conspirator, the unchecked wind off the Atlantic Ocean. Says Tom Watson, "It's a complete golf course with every type of hole. It's also unprotected. Given any type of wind, scoring could be very difficult."

Perhaps one reason for its merciless character in trying conditions is that Shinnecock Hills routing works in so many different directions. Only twice do holes run the same direction. That challenge is immediately apparent with the first three holes of the day, running in three different directions. In addition to the testing first, the second is an uphill par 3 of 226 yards to a green defended by six bunkers, while the third is a monster of 453 rolling yards with nine bunkers in play from tee to green.

Architect William Flynn has only recently been given full credit for the design of the final version of the course (replacing earlier designs from Willie Dunn in 1892 and C.B. MacDonald and Seth Raynor in 1913). While Flynn kept two of the MacDonald-Raynor holes, the oft-imitated Redan-style seventh hole and the plateaued green par-4 ninth, the wondrous variety of Shinnecock's menace is much Flynn's doing. He took full advantage of the 300 acres of land, running holes in every conceivable direction so the

wind becomes a constant battle. Nowhere is that more apparent than on the back nine where there is difficulty at every corner. The epic 10th, 12th and 14th holes are all classic par 4s where both length and accuracy are required. The short 11th and 17th demand precision to tiny exposed targets, while the 18th hole is a sweeping storm that demands a draw off the tee and a draw to the green. It is pure golf, the kind of challenge Ben Hogan applauded.

"It has not succumbed to the pattern of 'make golf easy' because of the hacker's inability to hit decent shots," he once wrote to a friend and Shinnecock member. "Each hole is different and requires a great amount of skill to play properly. Each hole has complete definition. You know exactly where to shoot. All in all, I think it is one of the finest courses I have ever played."

1973: Ben Crenshaw, playing a casual round at Shinnecock before turning pro, shoots 65, three better than the course record. The record is marked with an asterisk because Crenshaw took a mulligan off the first tee.

1986: Ray Floyd becomes the oldest U.S. Open winner in 66 years at age 43, finishing at one-under par for four rounds. At one point during the final round, nine players were tied for the lead at one-over par.

DEFINING MOMENTS

1977: The Walker Cup is played at Shinnecock Hills with the American side defeating Great Britain and Ireland 16–8. In the 16 singles matches played over two days, not a single player breaks par.

1995: Corey Pavin hits a majestic 4-wood through the wind and close to the pin on the closing hole to secure the 95th U.S. Open.

The climb to the 9th green is rewarded with a view of the finishing holes and a realization of the work at hand.

Feature Hole

 14

Named Thom's Elbow in honor of Charlie Thom, Shinnecock Hills' legendary head professional from 1906–61, the 14th is the rare hole here, guarded on nearly all sides by stands of scrub pines, which almost turn the fairway into a tiny sliver of a valley. Deep-faced bunkers guard both sides of the fairway, but as is true of nearly all of Shinnecock's longer holes, the green at the 14th is open in front to accept a running shot. Still, it is not unusual for the less than perfect shot to run all the way through the long, thinnish green here, because the hole typically plays downwind. In a rare northeasterly wind, like the one during the 1986 U.S. Open, the hole can be a bear. Said one member, "In a national Open, they have to play in any conditions, but when the wind blows from the northeast, the members stay in the bar."

444 YARDS

PAR 4

Southern Hills Country Club

Location: **Tulsa, Oklahoma**
Opened: **1936**
Architect: **Perry Maxwell**
Par: **71**
Length: **7,014 yards**

Southern Hills, that great championship test on the Southern plains, still reflects the character and tone of the time of its origin. Built during the depths of the Great Depression, the course is neither lavish, nor excessively contrived in any way, nor has it ever been mistaken for being quaint. Instead, it can be just as hard and mean as a dust storm, and about as straightforward as a bank foreclosure. It is not generally the sort of thing one conquers as much as survives, but the clarity of the task at hand, not to mention its requisite difficulty, is perhaps one reason Southern Hills has been the host site for seven major championships (three U.S. Opens, three PGA Championships and a U.S. Amateur) since 1958.

Despite its name, Southern Hills is not a course of dramatic elevation change. Although the first and 10th tees are elevated and the ninth and 18th greens are well above the fairway, the remainder of the course is more flattish than not. In short, the topography here does not lend itself to breather holes. Indeed, for championship play the only par 5s are the unreachable 655-yard fifth and the 537-yard 13th with water guarding the front of the green.

Southern Hills is a bull ride from the very beginning. The first three holes go 460, 471 and 405 yards, and that includes deep fairway bunkers on the first, a creek splitting the second fairway, and a sharp dogleg to a severely sloping green on the third. But nowhere is it tougher than on the final hole. The 18th plays 465 yards, slightly downhill at the start and then dramatically uphill at the finish to the wildest green on the course.

The mind gets a complete workout as the player contemplates all the options at Southern Hills. From the tee, the player is confronted with an array of doglegging longer holes. In fact, just two of the non-par-3 holes do not bend one way or the other, so players must not merely hit the

Twin ponds guard the green at the par-5 13th, tempering the aggressive strategy.

fairway, they must hit the right portion of the fairway. Six holes call for fades off the tee, while the other eight driving holes are best served by draws.

The shorter holes aren't layups, though. Each of the par 3s plays in a different direction, so the ever-present winds off the plains can cause their own set of hardships.

Perry Maxwell didn't stop working when he got to designing the putting surfaces at Southern Hills, either. Known for producing exceptional green contours during his redesign work at both Augusta National and Pine Valley, as well as his original work at Crystal Downs and Prairie Dunes, the famed "Maxwell Rolls," particularly at the third, ninth and 18th greens led Hale Irwin to once say, "You may hit it to six or seven feet of the hole on the greens here, and still have a tiger by the tail trying to two putt." Like many of the truly

great layouts, little of substance has changed to the Southern Hills design in almost 70 years. Perhaps this is because Maxwell did so little manufacturing of the golf course. But that was precisely his style. "The site of a golf course should be there, not brought there," Maxwell once said. "In this way, it will have its own character."

Thanks to his careful strokes, Southern Hills had the character of a champion at the start, and it still does to this moment. It is probably why Robert Trent Jones Sr., long lauded for his complete overhaul of potential U.S. Open venues, added barely a handful of bunkers when he was asked to upgrade Southern Hills prior to the 1958 U.S. Open. "You'd be a fool to let anyone make any further changes," he told the membership. "You've got one of the greatest golf courses in the world."

Feature Hole

Ben Hogan once referred to this hole as "the greatest par-4 12th hole in the United States." It's at least that good. A dogleg left with a fairway bunker in the inside of the elbow, the hole calls for a long draw off the tee to make use of the slope of the landing area. But players could be left with a slightly downhill lie to a green perched above a creek on the right side and guarded by bunkers on the left. In championship play, a miss short and right of the green often catches the shaved bank between the putting surface and the creek and the ball rolls into the hazard. In Tommy Bolt's victory in 1958, he birdied this brute three times, while the rest of the field played it in over par. The 12th typifies Southern Hills' nature, a place where, as former USGA president Sandy Tatum said: "The bold play is rewarded if the golfer can bring it off. But he is penalized if he cannot."

458 YARDS

PAR 4

The 18th demands two prodigious blows—and then a steady hand on the green.

1958: Tommy Bolt, long plagued by his tempestuous outbursts, played calm, controlled golf and won the 58th U.S. Open, his only major title, by four shots over Gary Player.

1994: Nick Price, whose 269 was the lowest score ever recorded in a major played at Southern Hills, records a sterling six-shot victory in the PGA Championship, his second consecutive major victory that year.

2001: Retief Goosen wins his first major title, overcoming a disastrous three-putt from 15 feet on the 72nd hole to beat Mark Brooks in a Monday playoff at the 101st U.S. Open.

DEFINING **MOMENTS**

1977: Hubert Green wins the U.S. Open by one shot over Lou Graham. Green was notified on the back nine that police had received a death threat against him, but when told, Green shrugged it off and played on.

Spyglass Hill Golf Course

Location: **Pebble Beach, California**
Opened: **1966**
Architect: **Robert Trent Jones Sr.**
Par: **72**
Length: **6,862 Yards**

The astounding scenery of Spyglass Hill's starting holes like the 2nd is tempered by its difficulty.

It is a vision in contrasts, but even as it changes in appearance and trimmings, its brutality remains the same. Spyglass Hill tends to be overlooked in the grand duchy of golfdom that is the Monterey Peninsula. With neighbors like Pebble Beach Golf Links and the Cypress Point Club, how could it not be? But the simple truth behind the genesis of Spyglass Hill is that its creator Robert Trent Jones Sr.. knew he was walking on hallowed golf ground, and so not just any old golf course would do. His mission was to take the contrasting dunesland and forest and make a course that was part Pine Valley and part Augusta National.

But the scenery at Spyglass Hill wasn't enough for Jones. He wanted more from the setting, more bunkers, more length, more water hazards, and presumably more despair, particularly for the tour players who would play it every January. That's why Bing Crosby bet Jack Nicklaus he wouldn't break par the first time Spyglass was inserted into the rotation of courses that make up what was then the Bing Crosby National Pro-Am. Der Bingle lost the bet, but only by a shot, as Nicklaus four-putted once and on another occasion saw a putt roll off the green and into a nearby pond.

Spyglass' initial severity actually had to be tempered before the next tournament, a severity that legendary chronicler Jim Murray once explained this way: "If it were human, Spyglass Hill would have a knife in its teeth, a patch on its eye, a ring in its ear, tobacco in its beard. It is a privateer plundering the golfing main, an amphibious creature, half ocean, half forest. It's a 200-acre unplayable lie."

The course is themed around Robert Louis Stevenson's famed tale *Treasure Island*, and each hole is named after elements and characters in the book. The course has a similar rhythm to the story: horror and near death on all sides at the start, followed by a series of challenges hidden up in the high woods. The first five holes at Spyglass Hill play to a backdrop of the roiling Pacific. It is a quick, epic trip, especially at holes like the par-3 third, which plays just 152 yards down to a smallish green on the verge of being swallowed up by the surf. Here the game off the tee can be unmerciful, as shots that miss greens or fairways routinely end up in gnarly, debilitating ice plant.

But after the sixth tee, the golf course turns inland and up the hill. The change to a parkland-style layout might otherwise seem benign, until you play it. Stands of Monterey pine trees along the sides of fairways punish misplayed shots. You have left the sand and ice plant, but now you must negotiate the even less forgiving ponds that guard a third of the remaining greens. Particularly memorable are the par-3 12th and 15th holes, where a water hazard guards the left edge of the green on the former and the right edge on the latter.

Devilishly, Jones thwarts the safe play on both holes with extra bunkering beyond the green. Adding to the mix of meanness are meatier holes, like the double-dogleg par-5 14th, again with water guarding the green, and the 16th, the longest par-4 at 464 yards with only one bunker, placed right in front of the green. The greens themselves have slopes on more of an edge than the earlier seaside holes. In fact, that edge was so strong originally that after Spyglass Hill's debut at the Crosby in 1967, six greens had to be redone.

Jones was pleased with the diversity of Spyglass Hill, calling it one of the five favorite designs of his career. He also was pleased with its difficulty, which remains its—and his—hallmark. "I wanted to make it the best and toughest test of golf on the Monterey Peninsula," he once said, "and I think we succeeded."

1967: Spyglass Hill becomes part of the rotation of courses used for the Bing Crosby National Pro Am and Jack Nicklaus' 71 goes a long way toward his five-stroke victory over Billy Casper.

1993: Dan Forsman (below) shoots a course-record 64, which is later equalled by Steve Lowery in 1995.

1998 The AT&T became perhaps the longest PGA event ever played. The final round was held six months after the tournament began because El Niño-powered rain washed out play. The tournament was won by Phil Mickelson.

DEFINING **MOMENTS**

1999: Payne Stewart wins the AT&T Pebble Beach National Pro-Am. Stewart, knowing the forecast for the final day was dire, birdied his final hole of the third round at Spyglass Hill to take a one-stroke lead and the eventual win.

Spyglass changes face at the 6th hole, but not its intensity.

Feature Hole

4

Robert Trent Jones Sr. only said this was the best par-4 hole he ever designed. The fairway here is a snaking island surrounded by sand and impossible recovery shots. But hitting the fairway only reveals a green that appears no wider than an exclamation point. The longer you hit the ball off the tee, the narrower the landing area gets and the scarier the hole plays. Jones forces the big driver to choose between pinpoint accuracy and safety, but choosing safety only then puts more of a squeeze on the approach shot. Not only that, the hole calls for a draw from the tee, but hit too much of one and the ice plant may cause you to lose both your ball and your will to continue. Adding to the fun is a two-tiered green. Fittingly, the hole is named Blind Pew after the crotchedy blind beggar who delivers the fateful Black Spot of imminent death to Billy Bones.

370 YARDS

PAR 4

The Cascades

Location: **Hot Springs, Virginia**
Opened: **1924**
Architect: **William Flynn**
Par: **70**
Length: **6,679 yards**

It is not easy to get to The Homestead Resort. From whatever direction you come, you arrive on back roads that climb and turn with every hillside and mountain stream. But then real treasures are not found on every street corner, and The Homestead's classic layout, The Cascades, is just such a gem.

A classically historic, heroic course that seems to have been sitting in a valley in the Allegheny Mountains for centuries, The Cascades is regarded by many as the finest mountainside course in America. If it is that, though, it is only so because William Flynn's design incorporated the topography gently, almost surreptitiously at times. Never once do you feel a particular play is being forced upon you by the land. And yet forget where you are and how it influences every shot and every decision, and you will most certainly lose your step.

"There isn't any kind of hill you don't have to play from or any kind of shot you won't hit there," said Sam Snead, who grew up just outside the door of the resort. "If you could train a youngster to play on that course, he'll play anywhere."

Snead would know. His game traveled pretty well after growing up here. Snead, who you might remember won a few Masters tournaments in Georgia in his time, would ultimately call The Cascades the finest course in the South, and while that may be a debatable point, there is little to mark against Flynn's Virginia design.

While there are no particularly epic uphill and downhill shots, the mountains seem to linger in the background of the entire round here. In truth, no single element dominates the layout. While there are an assorted number of blind drives and approaches (perhaps a clear example that Flynn let the golf course find the land), what remains consistent is the variety here. The danger area moves from left to right almost rhythmically throughout the round. (For instance, you cannot be left on four, right on six, 10 or 11, or left on 12, 13 or 17.) Not overly long (only four holes play longer than

With the stream on the right in play from the landing area to green, the par–5 17th is dangerous fun.

430 yards), and several par 4s do not even require a driver while another, the tiny 3rd, is reachable in one big hit. What is more, there is a bit of fun to the finish. After three of the toughest par 4s on the course (Nos. 12, 13 and 14), Flynn sandwiches two testing and lengthy par 3s around two tempting and shorter par 5s. The Cascades' overriding strength is its softer moments, though. For instance, the five par 3s move in four different directions and the greens are confounding, as Flynn was able to engineer breaks that seem to go against the flow of the landscape and play tricks on the eyes. It is this which prompted Snead to say, "It's the most complete test of golf I know. You have to hit every shot—the drive, long irons, fairway woods, pitches over water, sidehill, uphill, downhill lies, long and short trap shots—everything!"

Although a mountain course might typically bring thoughts of grandeur, and while the vistas here are memorable, the course itself hardly feels overly grand and bombastic. Instead, its design is cozy, intimate, yet it cannot be overcome merely with sheer strength, only with relentless precision. And yet in an odd way, many players find the challenge is mediated by an almost calming, relaxing feeling playing in these mountains can bring. It is those twin virtues that Flynn saw the first time he toured the property to draw up his course, and it is those he delivered, as well. "I have 20 locations where I can put a putting green," he said in 1923. "I don't know how the holes will run, but I can build you a course. It is going to cost money and take engineering, but I believe you will have an outstanding course and certainly one of the most beautiful anywhere."

Feature Hole

As good a par 4 as there is in golf and a hole once selected by Arnold Palmer as one of his all-time favorites, the 12th runs between a hillside and a mountain stream. The hole turns left and demands a draw from an elevated tee. Anything less than perfect from the tee will leave you with the issue of cross bunkers that crop up 90 yards short of the green. The hole illustrates just how Flynn let the holes at The Cascades happen, nudging them to near perfection. Here, the long iron second must be precise to a narrow green. But if the player is hesitant over his second, even his layup is challenged.

476 YARDS

PAR 4

The dramatic downhill par–3 4th displays as much substance as style.

1928: Glenna Collett (later Vare), perhaps the female equivalent of Bobby Jones, won the third of her six U.S. Women's Amateur titles, defeating Virginia Van Wie 13 & 12, the most lopsided margin for the next 33 years.

2000: Greg Puga, a 29-year-old caddie at Bel-Air Country Club in Los Angeles, becomes the youngest ever winner of the U.S. Mid-Amateur title, defeating Wayne Raath of South Africa, 3 & 1.

DEFINING MOMENTS

1966: With an experienced squad, including five-time veteran Barbara McIntire, the U.S. defeats the Great Britain and Ireland side in the Curtis Cup, 13–5.

1967: In a shocking upset, French woman Catherine Lacoste, daughter of tennis great Rene Lacoste, wins the U.S. Women's Open, becoming the first and only amateur ever to claim the title.

Miss the fairway
and the bunkers
near the 15th
green seem to
get bigger.

The Country Club

Location:	**Brookline, Massachusetts**
Opened:	**1893**
Architect:	**Willie & Alex Campbell/William Flynn**
Par:	**71**
Length:	**7,033 yards**

The Country Club will always be regarded as an American original. It was one of the famous first five clubs in American golf. As host site for the 1913 U.S. Open, it witnessed the shocking win by a 20-year-old local amateur that jump-started the popularity of the game in America. And in the 1999 Ryder Cup, it was the home course advantage in an epic American comeback. Like its home country, The Country Club can be seen as a hodge-podge collection, but unified, that whole presents a much greater force than the sum of its parts.

Though they were constructed at different times and have involved the opinions of at least seven different architects over the years, the three nines at The Country Club—the Clyde, Squirrel and the Primrose—reflect a similar image. It is a picture of the game at its earliest stages in the United States, where course design wasn't the blank-slate and open-checkbook style so commonly practiced in more modern designs. Here, the land dictated the holes. And so did the checkbook, or lack thereof. When a couple of members of The Country Club first set about building six holes for golf in the 1890s, they were granted permission from the board of governors, provided that construction costs were held under $50. That design is still very much alive in today's course, thanks to the efforts of architect Rees Jones, whose restoration for the 1988 U.S. Open was roundly praised. What is apparent is a no-nonsense approach where obstacles could not be circumvented or obliterated, only incorporated. If a rock outcropping blocked the line of sight from the tee, if an approach shot ended up being semi-blind, if a green seemed much too small, or even if a hole found itself in the middle of a horse racetrack (as was the case on the 18th hole) it didn't matter. The golf didn't change the landscape, it simply became part of it. The result is a course that produces great moments and great possibility.

Just like the reserved but posh suburb of Boston that is its home, The Country Club's course is understated elegance, as well. Holes march through wide open areas between stands of trees and around walls of rock. Tall fescue rough and perfectly positioned sand bunkers stand guard with a straightforward look that might make the course seem almost easy at first glance. Of course, it isn't. Francis Ouimet, the young American who defeated the great Britons Harry Vardon and Ted Ray in a playoff at the 1913 U.S. Open, once told his Walker Cup team as they prepared for the 1932 matches at Brookline, "Gentlemen, this is a very subtle course."

The championship course combines 15 holes of the original 18, with four holes from William Flynn's Primrose nine (two holes are combined into one to make the stout 450-yard 11th). But it does not pound away at you senselessly. Instead, it bounces along, begging you to drive two of the first five par 4s and asking for your courage on a drive around or over a rocky ledge on the par-5 ninth, known as "the Himalayas." It gets nasty after the turn with the three interloping holes from the Primrose, but the turn for home calls for precise shots to tight fairways and sloping greens.

Sixty-seven years after Ouimet counseled an American team about Brookline's underlying difficulty, Ben Crenshaw would do the same at the 1999 Ryder Cup.

"It tests your approaching ability from all angles, with all sorts of looks," said Crenshaw. "The greens have beautiful, natural undulations, which are very, very difficult to pick up sometimes. They are anything but straightforward. This is a course that requires a lot of knowing."

1913: Francis Ouimet, a local 20-year-old amateur, stuns the golf world and energizes golf in America with a playoff victory over the world's top two professionals, J.H. Taylor and Harry Vardon.

1988: Curtis Strange gets up and down from the deep bunker guarding the 18th green to force a Monday playoff with Nick Faldo in the U.S. Open, which Strange wins by four shots.

1999: Justin Leonard makes a miraculous 40-foot birdie putt to secure a precious half-point and complete the stunning U.S. comeback victory over Europe in the 33rd Ryder Cup matches.

DEFINING MOMENTS

1963: Julius Boros overcomes windy conditions and tough scoring to win the 63rd U.S. Open in a playoff against Arnold Palmer and Jacky Cupit. The 72-hole score of 293 was the highest since 1935.

The 3rd's horrors include mounds that obscure the green, an unseen road and a looming water hazard.

Feature Hole

17

It can be argued that no single hole has done so much for the collective heartbeat of American golf fans as the 17th at Brookline. A classic par 4, the dogleg left forces a decision from the tee and the bunker guarding the bend in the dogleg complicates that decision. A long, narrow and now wickedly two-tiered green further compounds the headache. It was here that Ouimet made a birdie that earned him a spot in a playoff with Vardon and Ray in the 1913 U.S. Open. The next day Vardon's drive ended up in the bunker, propelling Ouimet to his victory. It also led to a crucial Arnold Palmer bogey in the 1963 U.S. Open, and a Julius Boros one-putt that helped him win the title. And, of course, it was here that Justin Leonard's 40-foot birdie stunned the world and clinched an incredible U.S. comeback victory in the 1999 Ryder Cup.

370 YARDS
PAR 4

The Golf Club

Location: **New Albany, Ohio**
Opened: **1967**
Architect: **Pete Dye**
Par: **72**
Length: **7,268 yards**

Fred Jones was strictly no-nonsense when he set about trying to establish a men-only retreat in the land around Columbus, Ohio. His principles were direct and simple. Of the organization, he said, the club will be private. "We are going to have a club just for men. There will be no women, no kids and no dogs." Of the golf course, his direction was even more concise: "I want this course to look like it's been here forever as soon as it's finished."

Pete Dye took those instructions to heart, moved minimal earth in fashioning 18 distinct and separate holes and produced the kind of design that has become an American legend. While The Golf Club remains, in many ways, a hidden gem and by club mandate will never host an outside tournament, its images and lines emphasize principles that the great architects always manage to find in nature. The Golf Club epitomizes the way the difficulty of the game comfortably coexists with its natural beauty.

Jones gave the relatively inexperienced (at the time) Dye more than 400 acres, told him not to worry about the bills, and set him loose. Dye used a combination of different grasses, bent in the fairways and native fescues in the rough areas, to give the course what he once described in the club's history as a rugged "Old English" look, "maybe like the type Donald Ross or Mackenzie would design."

Indeed, while much of the prevailing golf course architecture of the same vintage emphasized a manicured wall-to-wall green look, The Golf Club exudes a wild feel with its contrasting hues of greens and browns and yellows. The contrast itself almost enhances the difficulty, further emphasizing in the golfer's mind the difference between fairway and rough.

With so much land at his disposal, Dye could incorporate the winding Blacklick Creek in the most ideal ways. While water is fully in play on 10 holes, only on the eighth and 18th is there any mandated carry of significant yardage. In the case of the former, it is the shortest par 3 totalling just 135 yards; while on the finisher, a good drive from an

Pete Dye's trademark railroad tie bunkers first took hold at The Golf Club's 3rd hole.

elevated tee should leave only a middle iron at most to the green.

What Dye always managed to do is to find the right amount of tilt to a green, the right sharpness of angle on a dogleg and the right type of bunker to challenge the particular shot required. Indeed, though there are only 49 bunkers on the course, there seems to be twice that many. Huge cross bunkers on holes like Nos. 2, 5, 14 and 15 seem to make fairways not merely shrink, but disappear entirely. Dye used mounding to add to the uncertainty at a hole like the 449-yard 15th, where the proper angle to attack the green is on the left side of the fairway, yet the only way to get there is to go directly over the fescue-strewn mounds in the cross bunker.

There are, of course, many other treats to The Golf Club's design, particularly the back-to-back stout par 4s at Nos. 5 and 6, which, combined, play longer than 900 yards. The sixth is notable for its two crossings of Blacklick Creek, both of which are fashioned out of abandoned railroad cars. There's also a steer skull placed in the waste bunker on the second hole and a hangman's noose on the unforgiving par-3 16th, put there after Jones once remarked after a particularly rough effort, "There ought to be a quick way to end it all, right here."

The Golf Club is a masterful collection of contrasts. As honorary member Jack Nicklaus once related in the club history, "It is marvellous and well-balanced. And no hole resembles any other on the course. When I first saw the course, I realized that Pete Dye was the most imaginative and innovative golf course designer of the period."

Feature Hole

13

In a golf course that fits so naturally with its surroundings, the 13th might strike some as a bit of an abrupt departure with wooden pilings lining both the raised fairway and framing the massive greenside bunker on the right. But here Dye employs some of the lessons he learned from visiting the great courses of Scotland. He suggests the 13th is inspired by the closing hole at Prestwick, and here the strong player is tempted to carry the waste area and the pilings to leave a short, unobstructed flick to the green. Play your tee ball safely to the right, however, and the angle for your second shot narrows the opening to the green and brings both the bunker and the pond left and right into play. Dye's command of the property makes the 13th not merely an effective transition between the 12th and 14th holes, but perhaps the highlight of the three.

369 YARDS

PAR 4

The long, watery 17th elicits aggression but demands fastidiousness.

1963: Eventual founder, Fred Jones, announces his intentions to build a men's-only club for his friends. When asked what the place would be called, he says, "Naturally, the only thing you would call it: The Golf Club."

1969: Just two years after it first opened for play, The Golf Club debuts in the top 40 on *Golf Digest*'s ranking of America's 100 Greatest Courses.

1999: The Golf Club is ranked 23rd in *Golf Digest*'s America's 100 Greatest Courses, its highest position on the list. It is the highest ranked Pete Dye course on the list.

DEFINING MOMENTS

1967: The Club opens in June and Fred Jones is presented with the Paul R. Shipman Trophy for his "dedication to the Club, his sportsmanship and the contribution he has made to the welfare and fellowship of the members."

The Olympic Club (Lake)

Location: **San Francisco, California**
Opened: **1928**
Architect: **Sam Whiting**
Par: **71**
Length: **6,842**

The character of the Lakeside Course at San Francisco's Olympic Club mirrors that of the game itself. It continually does its level best to temper, sometimes even destroy, your sense of self-confidence. Almost at every turn of this heavily wooded parkland-style layout just this side of the street from the Pacific Ocean, the player remains awash in uncertainty, unable to find his footing and not only because he's facing an awkward stance.

The unbalanced stance at Olympic is an unavoidable result for even the well-played shot. It is not unusual here for a hole to move from right to left, while the fairway slopes the opposite way. Indeed, not only is it not unusual, it is in very many ways Olympic's hallmark.

Such confounding slopes make precision paramount. Players must not only hit precise spots off the tee, but their ballflights must be specifically geared to counteract the negative effects of the sloping landing areas. But, of course, that's only half the game at Olympic. The challenge is further exacerbated by 40,000 firs, eucalyptus, redwoods and Monterey pines that were originally planted by the course's construction supervisor, head pro and ultimately the man deservedly given the lion's share of the credit for Olympic's design, Sam Whiting. Ironically, the trees were Whiting's effort to protect golfers from the ocean breezes that could plague the Lake course. Today, of course, those sentries lining each fairway make the course play bigger than its 6,800 yards. Ben Hogan, the man who was stunningly defeated at Olympic in a playoff with Jack Fleck, summed it up this way, "Olympic is the longest short course in the world."

As if the trees, the narrow, sloping fairways and the ever-present wind weren't enough to shake even the steadiest of hands, Olympic's final insult are its tiny greens, often protected by scalloped bunkers that constrict and perplex whether you're standing in one of them or eyeing one from a distance. All but two of Olympic's greens are guarded by significant bunkering.

In the end, there is a certain repetitive obstinancy to Olympic's pacing, too; the kind of experience that frankly didn't exactly charm Jack Nicklaus, who once said, "It's monotonous. There's no water, no out-of-bounds, you just plod along and play golf."

But don't think for a minute that the day is boring. It's roller coaster fairways are relentless, and while the day starts safely enough with a downhill par 5, the early part of the course is a series of body blows designed to disable any swagger in your step. From the second hole through the sixth, the run includes a 223-yard par 3 and four par 4s that average over 430 yards. Said Ben Crenshaw, "Playing holes three, four, five and six is like walking through a minefield."

But just when you are winded, Olympic teases you with a driveable par 4 and the shortest par 3 on the course. The onslaught continues all through the back nine. Holes like 14 and 16 are best navigated with safe tee shots giving way to longer, but just as conservatively played, approach shots. The par-5 16th is unreachable, while the 17th hole is a converted par 4 for championship play where even five is not a certainty. Even on the short 18th, wedge shots are to a green canted and sloping enough to be nearly unputtable, as it was for a particular back left pin position at the 1998 U.S. Open.

Clearly, the Lake course is all about unforgiving precision. There is a reason that in its three U.S. Opens the best winning 72-hole score was merely two-under par. As Tom Kite once reflected, "It's a dynamite course. It makes you hit the shots. If you don't, it will kill you."

1955: Unheralded Jack Fleck birdies the 72nd hole to tie Ben Hogan on 287 in the 55th U.S. Open. Fleck comes to the 18th hole of the playoff with a one-stroke lead and calmly makes par over Hogan's six to win.

1958: Charlie Coe wins four matches that come down to the final three holes in claiming his second U.S. Amateur. In the field were future stars Tommy Aaron, Deane Beman, Al Geiberger and a young Jack Nicklaus.

1966: Arnold Palmer, leading the U.S. Open by seven shots on the 10th tee, squanders his lead to fall into a tie with his playing companion Billy Casper. In the playoff, Casper rallies on the back nine to outplay Palmer, 69–73.

DEFINING
MOMENTS

1981: Nathaniel Crosby, teenaged son of singer Bing Crosby, wins the U.S. Amateur, rallying from four down with 10 holes to play to defeat Brian Lindley on the first extra hole with a 20-foot birdie putt.

The trees at holes like 14 were planted to protect golfers; now they confound them.

Feature Hole

Hardly much more than a long iron and a wedge, Olympic's 18th hole baits you into believing in a closing birdie. But the shot off the tee becomes more difficult the longer it carries, and the shot to the green is so much more than a little flick. Uphill to a long, thin green, there is no safe miss here. With the pin at the back, players risk going over the green and leaving themselves an impossible chip from a downhill lie to a green sloping away. When the pin is up front, the need to keep the ball short of the pin brings every bunker into play. Some say the bunkers around the 18th green seem to spell out the letters I-O-U. It is the final bit of evidence that Olympic's Lake Course always manages to have the last laugh.

347 YARDS

PAR 4

TPC at Sawgrass (Stadium)

Location: **Ponte Vedra Beach, Florida**
Opened: **1981**
Architect: **Pete Dye**
Par: **72**
Length: **6,954 yards**

Was the Stadium Course at the Tournament Players Club at Sawgrass pure genius or pure evil? In the mind of architect Pete Dye, it may have been both—a case of inspired torture, as it were. Today, you can almost hear the cackle in Dye's voice when he talks about his efforts. "I wanted to test the best players in the world emotionally as well as physically and mentally."

In a way, that triumvirate of tests lies at the very nature of the game. At the Stadium Course, Dye took that theme and set it in a theater. The primary motivation for the project initially was to create a course where the spectator could see more of the action on every hole. But Dye, of course, did much more than fabricate natural bleachers. He gave the assembled fans something to look at, too, and occasionally the view was of a crash scene with multiple injuries. Even without the enhanced spectator positions, though, the Stadium Course is a masterstroke of strategy and execution, of options and imperatives, of fear and fortitude. Dye worked to make the course especially demanding to the best players, but less than brutal for average golfers. He is quick to point out, for instance, that all but three of the greens accept run-up shots, and only one, the infamous 17th, has a substantial forced carry over water.

It has been called target golf, penal architecture and even the "Palace of Pain" by one professional golfer, but today the Stadium Course intrigues at least as much as it infuriates. There are four par 4s under 400 yards, but five stretch to 440 yards or more in length. Three of the par 5s can be reached, but only with heroic shots, and when the wind is up, the most difficult hole on the property might be the shortest.

Dye lets the round build magically to one of the best finishing stretches in golf. The front nine highlights include the big fifth hole, the second longest par 4 on the course

At No. 16, the temptation to score can produce troubling results.

with its tabletop fairway and a green that demands a fade. It is followed by a green looking for a hook at No. 7 and the sometimes-reachable par-5 ninth. Dye, under the advice of Deane Beman, tried to keep the first and 10th holes relatively similar, so a player teeing off from the 10th hole would not get an advantage in tournament play.

But after the deliciously adventurous par–5 11th hole, Dye picks up the day's intensity. At the wicked short par-4 12th, a tee ball that finds itself in the left half of the fairway may lead to a blind second over deep mounds. It is followed by an exacting par 3, with water lurking on the left edge of the green and a bunker most humans cannot play out of on the right side of the green. Then comes the hardest par 4 on the course, setting the stage for three startling finishing holes, where anything from eagle to double bogey is

possible. The 16th is a classic risk-reward par 5, the 17th is the show-stealing island-green par 3, and the 18th is a classic punishing par-4 finisher, where a tee ball left is wet and one to the right almost always results in bogey.

The Stadium Course was a jolt to the system for Tour players and their grousing actually originally softened it after its first year of play. Later, however, they called for it to be toughened up, reflecting the desire to be challenged in every way that every golfer knows and insists upon. Dye knows what lies at the golfer's soul; the Stadium Course merely feeds it. "I can't explain it, but that place just has a feel about it and a lot of people pick up on that feel," he once said. "They just want to go play that thing, even if they know they're going to get their brains beat in by it."

Feature Hole

17

Rightly or wrongly, it has become the definitive statement of Pete Dye's masterpiece at the Stadium Course. But the strange truth about the 17th is that it wasn't supposed to be that type of hole. As construction of the course went on around it and more of the sandy soil surrounding the green was removed for use on other parts of the course, the waste area began to take shape as a pond, whereupon Dye's wife and architect partner Alice suggested the island green. Rarely requiring more than an 8- or 9-iron, the hole lingers in the player's mind throughout his entire round. Exposed to the wind and with no options other than hitting the green, the 17th is a psychological masterstroke. A ridge running through the green, which is about 20 percent smaller than the average green on the course, can make the tiny target even more demanding. Says Sergio Garcia, "It gets in your head. That's good."

132 YARDS

PAR 3

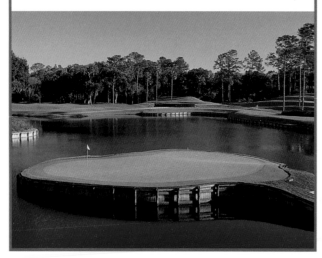

The options and possibilities of the par–5 11th make it one of the many surprises at Sawgrass.

1982: With Jack Nicklaus leading the critics, the course debuts at the Players Championship. Jerry Pate wins and then tosses both PGA Tour commissioner Deane Beman and architect Pete Dye into the lake by the 18th green.

2000: Seventeen years after he won his first Players Championship, Hal Sutton stares down world No. 1 Tiger Woods and wins his second title, shooting a four-round total of 278, one stroke better than Woods.

DEFINING MOMENTS

1994: With a birdie on the 35th hole, Tiger Woods becomes the youngest winner of the U.S. Amateur at age 18, defeating Trip Kuehne two up. Six down at one point, Woods wins six of the final 10 holes.

2002: Previously unheralded Craig Perks makes the Players Championship his first career victory, bouncing in two chip shots and a 25-foot birdie putt in the final three holes.

Not a blade of grass is wasted, not an angle unused on Wannamoisett's tiny plot.

Wannamoisett Country Club

Location: **Rumford, Rhode Island**
Opened: **1914**
Architect: **Donald Ross (1926)**
Par: **69**
Length: **6,661 yards**

Tucked at the end of a quiet side street, Wannamoisett Country Club stands considerably larger than the sum of its parts. It plays to only a par of 69, the lowest such figure in *Golf Digest's* ranking of America's 100 greatest courses. Its scorecard adds up to only about 6,600 yards, never to expand beyond that. Its site, quaint as it is, only encompasses 104 acres, barely enough for some courses front nines these days. But those aggregate figures short change this magnificently compact gem's true value. Hole by hole, shot by shot, moment by moment, Wannamoisett stands as tall as any course built on twice the space.

Donald Ross was reportedly pleased with his effort at maximizing the minimal space available to him. In the biography *Discovering Donald Ross* he is noted to have said, "This is the best layout I ever made, a fine course on 100 acres of land, no congestion, fine variety."

Of course, "fine variety" does not even remotely begin to describe Wannamoisett's thorough challenge and crafted intricacy. More than 100 bunkers dot the landscape here, at first blush almost randomly placed but then, upon further inspection, a clearly calculated marvel. Wannamoisett clearly illustrates Ross' professed philosophy on sand, namely, "There is no such thing as a misplaced bunker," he once said. "Regardless of where a bunker may be, it is the business of the player to avoid it."

No less a historian of golf course architecture and the game than Ben Crenshaw once called Wannamoisett "an architectural masterpiece." But then Gentle Ben certainly had a genuine affection for the tiny giant, having won the prestigious Northeast Amateur at Wannamoisett in 1973. This select championship (winners include Jay Sigel, John Cook and Hal Sutton) has helped Wannamoisett get the national attention it richly deserves.

What is truly amazing about Wannamoisett is how Ross

was able to produce so much variety and intrigue, so much subtlety and, at the same, time brute force on such a simple little square of property. There is just enough diversity in the landscape to keep the average player honest, while demanding something special from the elite player attempting to score boldly. For instance, Ross hides a little stream at the brawny 474-yard second hole, where anything less than a good drive brings a measure of uncertainty for the approach shot—and even then there are doubts. There's a grand punch-bowl setting for the green on the uphill 10th hole, and the deep wide bunker fronting the par-3 12th green makes it as striking a short uphill hole as there is in golf. And even though there are eight holes that parallel one another, each remains a distinct and unique challenge.

But Ross does more than simply work the land—he works the mind, too. Everywhere there are possibilities. Some long holes, like the first, provide the chance to run the ball onto the green, while others, like the second and ninth, are clearly heroic in nature. The short par 4s, particularly the tightly bunkered fifth and seventh holes, and the daring right-angle dogleg, pond-protected 14th, almost always demand an extra degree of precision both off the tee and from the fairway. All of this is typical of Ross, who once said of drive-and-pitch holes, "Both the drive and and pitch should be difficult. Otherwise, they are usually very uninteresting."

Wannamoisett never could be accused of being uninteresting. It never gets complacent, never underachieves. It may be a trifle small in stature, but it plays extra large.

1926: Donald Ross returns to strengthen the bunkering from his original design of the course done in 1914. He keeps the routing essentially unchanged and from that time until the present the course remains unaltered.

1962: The club begins the Northeast Amateur, an invitational stroke play event and British Amateur champion Dick Siderowf wins with a three-over three-day total.

DEFINING MOMENTS

1931: Unheralded pro Tom Creavy stuns a field that includes Walter Hagen, Tommy Armour and Gene Sarazen (the medalist) to win the 14th PGA Championship, defeating Denny Shute in the final 2 & 1.

1979: Reigning U.S. Amateur champion John Cook wins his second straight Northeast Amateur, shooting a new course record 63 in the second round and eventually winning by nine shots.

Feature Hole

The short par 3 is a dying art form, but Ross shows why it can be such a powerful force with this nugget. Ross had a simple rule for one-shotters: "Make all the short holes difficult." That's precisely what he accomplished right under the golfer's nose at the third hole. Wonderfully placed within the round, the third follows more than 900 yards of back-to-back par 4s. So Ross toys with the golfer's psyche, letting him think he might be getting something back with a short hole, only to find a hole that might prove even more damaging to the scorecard than its predecessor, which was nearly four times as long. What Ross referred to as "scooped-out pits" of sand guard a green perched on a tiny plateau. The hole's design is so well-regarded as being emblematic of Ross's style, that the Donald Ross Society uses a rendering of it as their organization's logo.

138 YARDS

PAR 3

The more the pond at No. 14 is successfully challenged, the better the options are for the second shot.

Winged Foot Golf Club (West)

Location: **Mamaroneck, New York**
Opened: **1923**
Architect: **A.W. Tillinghast**
Par: **72**
Length: **6,956 yards**

The legendary instructions given to A.W. Tillinghast, on embarking on the design project for the 36 holes that would become Winged Foot Golf Club, were simple but dramatic: "Give us a man-sized golf course." Looking at what his efforts produced at the West Course, you are left to wonder if the man Tillinghast had in mind was Paul Bunyan. It's not merely that Winged Foot West is a behemoth, it's that the challenge of navigating your way around its rough, its deep greenside bunkers and its unyielding greens is as large as all of golf can offer.

As Tillinghast himself later summarized, the West Course initially requires only two things, both of them monumentally difficult: "The key to scoring over Winged Foot is the consistent play at hard-hit, accurate seconds to the greens, and incidentally, the constant driving out far enough to get home under control." He didn't mention the greens, of course. But he easily could have. Many have a grade of three to four percent from front to back, meaning almost certain disaster to the man who overplays his approach shot.

Winged Foot is often stereotyped as an Anvil Chorus of monstrous par 4s. That would be slightly incomplete and mostly true at the same time. Certainly, Winged Foot's par 4s are a sturdy lot. Six of them play longer than 430 yards, and that number becomes eight for championship play when the par-5 ninth and 16th holes are converted to par 4s.

But Winged Foot West also reveals a stirring collection of par 3 holes, arguably the best foursome of short holes on a Tillinghast course. In addition, the tiny par-4 sixth is a perfect example of finesse being rewarded over strength. The closer you get to the green the harder the hole plays, yet on a course like Winged Foot, which seemingly presents so few opportunities to score, the temptation to play boldly can cloud any player's judgment.

There is not a significant amount of water in play here,

The long 9th can be especially bearish when converted to a par–4.

just a stream on the 15th hole. But that is not to say Winged Foot West is without hazard. Its fairways are lined with a glut of trees that overhang the line of flight, distorting perception off the tee and making successful recovery shots that much less likely. But its bunkers are the most formidable defense here, pushing up at the sides of elevated greens and leaving players with so many decidedly unpleasant sand shots. Often, too, the bunkers squeeze the entryway to greens making them seem that much smaller than they really are. Says Ben Crenshaw, "No golf course calls for a greater variety of bunker shots."

Despite a site that presented little majesty, Winged Foot was destined for greatness the moment Tillinghast completed the project. Its holes demand the ability to move shots in either direction, both from the tee and the fairway. There are seven doglegs on the back nine alone. And its bunkers and greens are a relentless reminder that the challenge is not complete until the ball is removed from the hole.

Not surprisingly, perhaps, Winged Foot played host to its first major, the U.S. Open, just six years after it opened for play. Tillinghast warned the participants in the pages of *Golf Illustrated* at the time, writing, "The winner can only be a man who hits them far and true and who can stand the gaff from start to finish. The contouring of the greens places great premium on placement of drives, but never is there the necessity of facing a prodigious carry of the sink-or-swim sort. In fact, every hole, barring the one-shotters, seems quite innocent, and it is only the knowledge that the next shot must be played with rifle accuracy that brings the realization that the drive must be placed."

Feature Hole

10

Ben Hogan, only half jokingly, called it "a 3-iron into some guy's bedroom." Julius Boros once suggested the front right bunker was big enough to house a national park. And A.W. Tillinghast considered it only the finest par 3 he had ever built, while others have suggested it might be the best par 3 ever without a water hazard. The downhill one-shotter that starts the back nine can very nearly ruin one's enthusiasm for the remainder of the day. First, the hole is oriented differently than any other on the course, making judging wind direction difficult. Second, out-of-bounds lies just 30 feet over the green, which slopes severely from back left to front right. Third, the bunkers are deep and unforgiving. Fourth, the green might be the toughest on the course. In short, says Jack Nicklaus, "The hole is a very severe green to miss and a very severe green to putt."

190 YARDS

PAR 3

As seen at the second hole, **Winged Foot** seems always awash in shadows.

1929: Bobby Jones must make a curving 12-footer for par on the 18th hole to force a tie with Al Espinosa at the U.S. Open. The putt goes in and Jones goes on to win the 36-hole playoff by 23 strokes.

1974: Referred to as "the Massacre at Winged Foot," the 74th U.S. Open sees the field average over 76 strokes a round. Hale Irwin's winning four-round total was seven-over 287.

1997: Davis Love III, the son of a teaching pro, wins the PGA Championship by five shots with a final round 66, his third in four rounds of the tournament.

DEFINING
MOMENTS

1984: Greg Norman holes a 50-foot par putt on the 18th hole to finish in a tie with Fuzzy Zoeller, who endears himself to the crowd by waving a white towel in surrender. But Zoeller wins the playoff by eight shots.

Scorecards

AUGUSTA NATIONAL GOLF CLUB PAR: 72 YARDAGE: 7290

1	2	3	4	5	6	7	8	9	OUT
435	575	350	205	455	180	410	570	460	3640
4	5	4	3	4	3	4	5	4	36
10	11	12	13	14	15	16	17	18	IN
495	490	155	510	440	500	170	425	465	3650
4	4	3	5	4	5	3	4	4	36

BALTRUSOL GOLF CLUB (LOWER) PAR: 72 YARDAGE: 7221

1	2	3	4	5	6	7	8	9	OUT
478	381	466	195	413	470	505	374	205	3487
5	4	4	3	4	4	5	4	3	36
10	11	12	13	14	15	16	17	18	IN
454	428	218	401	415	430	216	630	542	3734
4	4	3	4	4	4	3	5	5	36

BAY HILL GOLF CLUB PAR: 72 YARDAGE: 7239

1	2	3	4	5	6	7	8	9	OUT
441	218	395	530	384	558	197	459	467	3649
4	3	4	5	4	5	3	4	4	36
10	11	12	13	14	15	16	17	18	IN
400	438	580	364	206	425	517	219	441	3590
4	4	5	4	3	4	5	3	4	36

BELLERIVE COUNTRY CLUB PAR: 72 YARDAGE: 7503

1	2	3	4	5	6	7	8	9	OUT
440	441	211	561	458	201	389	588	428	3717
4	4	3	5	4	3	4	5	4	36
10	11	12	13	14	15	16	17	18	IN
575	378	481	184	415	462	230	604	457	3786
5	4	4	3	4	4	3	5	4	36

BETHPAGE STATE PARK (BLACK) PAR: 71 YARDAGE: 7380

1	2	3	4	5	6	7	8	9	OUT
430	389	212	522	455	411	576	211	425	3631
4	4	3	5	4	4	5	3	4	36
10	11	12	13	14	15	16	17	18	IN
487	444	489	566	165	478	487	213	420	3749
4	4	4	5	3	4	4	3	4	35

CHICAGO GOLF CLUB PAR: 70 YARDAGE: 6574

1	2	3	4	5	6	7	8	9	OUT
450	440	219	536	320	395	207	413	406	3386
4	4	3	5	4	4	3	4	4	35
10	11	12	13	14	15	16	17	18	IN
139	410	414	149	351	393	525	382	425	3188
3	4	4	3	4	4	5	4	4	35

COLONIAL COUNTRY CLUB PAR: 70 YARDAGE: 7080

1	2	3	4	5	6	7	8	9	OUT
565	400	476	246	470	427	420	192	402	3571
5	4	4	3	4	4	4	3	4	35
10	11	12	13	14	15	16	17	18	IN
404	609	433	178	459	430	188	383	427	3509
4	5	4	3	4	4	3	4	4	35

CRYSTAL DOWNS GOLF CLUB PAR: 70 YARDAGE: 6518

1	2	3	4	5	6	7	8	9	OUT
460	425	191	409	353	384	335	550	175	3282
4	4	3	4	4	4	4	5	3	35
10	11	12	13	14	15	16	17	18	IN
395	196	430	442	147	327	588	311	400	3236
4	3	4	4	3	4	5	4	4	35

CYPRESS POINT CLUB PAR: 72 YARDAGE: 6536

1	2	3	4	5	6	7	8	9	OUT
421	548	162	384	493	518	168	363	292	3349
4	5	3	4	5	5	3	4	4	37
10	11	12	13	14	15	16	17	18	IN
480	437	404	365	388	143	231	393	346	3187
5	4	4	4	4	3	3	4	4	35

DESERT FOREST GOLF CLUB PAR: 72 YARDAGE: 7035

1	2	3	4	5	6	7	8	9	OUT
375	428	186	394	453	369	534	206	501	3446
4	4	3	4	4	4	5	3	5	36
10	11	12	13	14	15	16	17	18	IN
393	581	191	446	369	410	523	212	464	3589
4	5	3	4	4	4	5	3	4	36

EAST LAKE GOLF CLUB — PAR: 72 YARDAGE: 7196

1	2	3	4	5	6	7	8	9	OUT
424	195	387	440	561	164	394	405	584	3554
4	3	4	4	5	3	4	4	5	36

10	11	12	13	14	15	16	17	18	IN
516	193	391	439	442	495	481	453	232	3642
5	3	4	4	4	5	4	4	3	36

LOS ANGELES COUNTRY CLUB (NORTH) — PAR: 71 YARDAGE: 6909

1	2	3	4	5	6	7	8	9	OUT
523	548	386	203	478	355	235	558	176	3462
5	5	4	3	4	4	3	5	3	36

10	11	12	13	14	15	16	17	18	IN
374	245	371	455	556	132	445	430	439	3447
4	3	4	4	5	3	4	4	4	35

FIRESTONE COUNTRY CLUB (SOUTH) — PAR: 70 YARDAGE: 7139

1	2	3	4	5	6	7	8	9	OUT
399	497	442	458	200	469	219	450	470	3604
4	5	4	4	3	4	3	4	4	35

10	11	12	13	14	15	16	17	18	IN
410	370	178	457	418	221	625	392	464	3535
4	4	3	4	4	3	5	4	4	35

MAUNA KEA GOLF COURSE — PAR: 72 YARDAGE: 7165

1	2	3	4	5	6	7	8	9	OUT
383	394	261	413	593	344	204	530	427	3549
4	4	3	4	5	4	3	5	4	36

10	11	12	13	14	15	16	17	18	IN
554	247	387	409	413	201	422	555	428	3616
5	3	4	4	4	3	4	5	4	36

FISHERS ISLAND CLUB — PAR: 72 YARDAGE: 6566

1	2	3	4	5	6	7	8	9	OUT
396	172	335	397	229	520	363	465	364	3241
4	3	4	4	3	5	4	5	4	36

10	11	12	13	14	15	16	17	18	IN
401	164	389	400	425	533	146	415	452	3325
4	3	4	4	4	5	3	4	5	36

MEDINAH COUNTRY CLUB (NO. 3) — PAR: 72 YARDAGE: 7401

1	2	3	4	5	6	7	8	9	OUT
388	184	415	447	530	449	589	206	439	3647
4	3	4	4	5	4	5	3	4	36

10	11	12	13	14	15	16	17	18	IN
582	407	471	219	583	389	452	206	445	3754
5	4	4	3	5	4	4	3	4	36

GARDEN CITY GOLF CLUB — PAR: 73 YARDAGE: 6911

1	2	3	4	5	6	7	8	9	OUT
302	137	407	523	360	440	550	418	323	3460
4	3	4	5	4	4	5	4	4	37

10	11	12	13	14	15	16	17	18	IN
414	426	193	538	343	447	405	495	190	3451
4	4	3	5	4	4	4	5	3	36

MERION GOLF CLUB (EAST) — PAR: 70 YARDAGE: 6544

1	2	3	4	5	6	7	8	9	OUT
355	535	183	600	426	420	350	360	195	3424
4	5	3	5	4	4	4	4	3	36

10	11	12	13	14	15	16	17	18	IN
312	370	405	129	414	378	430	224	458	3120
4	4	4	3	4	4	4	3	4	34

HARBOUR TOWN GOLF LINKS — PAR: 71 YARDAGE: 6973

1	2	3	4	5	6	7	8	9	OUT
410	502	437	200	530	419	195	470	332	3495
4	5	4	3	5	4	3	4	4	36

10	11	12	13	14	15	16	17	18	IN
444	436	430	373	192	571	395	185	452	3478
4	4	4	4	3	5	4	3	4	35

MUIRFIELD VILLAGE GOLF CLUB — PAR: 72 YARDAGE: 7224

1	2	3	4	5	6	7	8	9	OUT
451	455	401	200	527	447	563	182	407	3633
4	4	4	3	5	4	5	3	4	36

10	11	12	13	14	15	16	17	18	IN
441	567	166	455	363	503	215	437	444	3591
4	5	3	4	4	5	3	4	4	36

INVERNESS CLUB — PAR: 71 YARDAGE: 7255

1	2	3	4	5	6	7	8	9	OUT
395	385	200	466	450	231	481	569	468	3645
4	4	3	4	4	3	4	5	4	35

10	11	12	13	14	15	16	17	18	IN
363	378	172	516	480	468	409	470	354	3610
4	4	3	5	4	4	4	4	4	36

NATIONAL GOLF LINKS OF AMERICA — PAR: 73 YARDAGE: 6873

1	2	3	4	5	6	7	8	9	OUT
327	330	426	195	478	141	478	424	540	3339
4	4	4	3	5	3	5	4	5	37

10	11	12	13	14	15	16	17	18	IN
450	432	435	174	365	397	404	375	502	3534
4	4	4	3	4	4	4	4	5	36

KIAWAH ISLAND (OCEAN COURSE) — PAR: 72 YARDAGE: 7296

1	2	3	4	5	6	7	8	9	OUT
395	528	390	432	207	455	527	197	464	3595
4	5	4	4	3	4	5	3	4	36

10	11	12	13	14	15	16	17	18	IN
439	562	466	404	194	421	579	197	439	3701
4	5	4	4	3	4	5	3	4	36

OAK HILL COUNTRY CLUB (EAST) — PAR: 71 YARDAGE: 7098

1	2	3	4	5	6	7	8	9	OUT
460	401	211	570	436	167	460	430	454	3599
4	4	3	5	4	3	4	4	4	35

10	11	12	13	14	15	16	17	18	IN
432	222	372	594	323	177	439	460	480	3499
4	3	4	5	4	3	4	5	4	36

OAKLAND HILLS COUNTRY CLUB (SOUTH) — PAR: 72 YARDAGE: 7105

1	2	3	4	5	6	7	8	9	OUT
435	523	198	430	465	360	411	482	220	3524
4	5	3	4	4	4	4	5	3	36

10	11	12	13	14	15	16	17	18	IN
453	423	561	171	473	401	406	201	492	3581
4	4	5	3	4	4	4	3	5	36

OAKMONT COUNTRY CLUB — PAR: 71 YARDAGE: 7230

1	2	3	4	5	6	7	8	9	OUT
483	341	426	614	383	196	501	253	481	3678
4	4	4	5	4	3	4	3	5	36

10	11	12	13	14	15	16	17	18	IN
463	382	625	185	360	502	233	315	487	3552
4	4	5	3	4	4	3	4	4	35

OLYMPIA FIELDS COUNTRY CLUB (NORTH) — PAR: 70 YARDAGE: 7177

1	2	3	4	5	6	7	8	9	OUT
580	471	461	400	417	187	430	247	445	3638
5	4	4	4	4	3	4	3	4	35

10	11	12	13	14	15	16	17	18	IN
444	402	387	168	444	576	215	433	468	3539
4	4	4	3	4	5	3	4	4	35

PEACHTREE GOLF CLUB — PAR: 72 YARDAGE: 7043

1	2	3	4	5	6	7	8	9	OUT
390	524	405	166	532	215	434	369	392	3427
4	5	4	3	5	3	4	4	4	36

10	11	12	13	14	15	16	17	18	IN
516	220	455	418	179	448	528	439	413	3616
5	3	4	4	3	4	5	4	4	36

PEBBLE BEACH GOLF LINKS — PAR: 72 YARDAGE: 6841

1	2	3	4	5	6	7	8	9	OUT
376	502	390	331	188	513	106	418	466	3290
4	5	4	4	3	5	3	4	4	36

10	11	12	13	14	15	16	17	18	IN
446	380	202	399	523	397	403	178	543	3551
4	4	3	4	5	4	4	3	5	36

PINEHURST RESORT & COUNTRY CLUB (NO. 2) — PAR: 71 YARDAGE: 7189

1	2	3	4	5	6	7	8	9	OUT
403	449	340	550	483	224	404	466	190	3509
4	4	4	5	4	3	4	4	3	35

10	11	12	13	14	15	16	17	18	IN
611	452	446	381	437	205	516	187	445	3680
5	4	4	4	4	3	5	3	4	36

PINE VALLEY GOLF CLUB — PAR: 70 YARDAGE: 6667

1	2	3	4	5	6	7	8	9	OUT
427	367	185	461	226	391	585	327	432	3401
4	4	3	4	3	4	5	4	4	35

10	11	12	13	14	15	16	17	18	IN
145	399	382	448	185	603	436	344	424	3366
3	4	4	4	3	5	4	4	4	35

PRAIRIE DUNES COUNTRY CLUB — PAR: 70 YARDAGE: 6598

1	2	3	4	5	6	7	8	9	OUT
432	161	355	168	438	387	512	430	426	3309
4	3	4	3	4	4	5	4	4	35

10	11	12	13	14	15	16	17	18	IN
185	452	390	395	370	200	415	500	382	3289
3	4	4	4	4	3	4	5	4	35

RIDGEWOOD COUNTRY CLUB — PAR: 35 (EAST); 36 (CENTER); 36 (WEST) YARDAGE: 3411 (EAST); 3345 (CENTER); 3534 (WEST)

EAST COURSE

1	2	3	4	5	6	7	8	9	OUT
375	177	567	414	407	229	460	403	379	3411
4	3	5	4	4	3	4	4	4	35

CENTER COURSE

1	2	3	4	5	6	7	8	9	OUT
370	563	458	530	216	289	396	143	380	3345
4	5	4	5	3	4	4	3	4	36

WEST COURSE

1	2	3	4	5	6	7	8	9	OUT
371	384	202	597	413	151	420	569	427	3534
4	4	3	5	4	3	4	5	4	36

RIVIERA COUNTRY CLUB — PAR: 71 YARDAGE: 7256

1	2	3	4	5	6	7	8	9	OUT
503	463	434	236	444	200	408	462	496	3646
5	4	4	3	4	3	4	4	4	35

10	11	12	13	14	15	16	17	18	IN
315	564	460	459	176	443	166	576	451	3610
4	5	4	4	3	4	3	5	4	36

SALEM COUNTRY CLUB — PAR: 72 YARDAGE: 6823

1	2	3	4	5	6	7	8	9	OUT
408	395	165	399	506	223	390	515	425	3426
4	4	3	4	5	3	4	5	4	36

10	11	12	13	14	15	16	17	18	IN
410	493	151	342	213	530	420	423	415	3397
4	5	3	4	3	5	4	4	4	36

SAND HILLS GOLF CLUB — PAR: 71 YARDAGE: 7089

1	2	3	4	5	6	7	8	9	OUT
549	458	216	485	412	198	283	367	402	3370
5	4	3	4	4	3	4	4	4	35

10	11	12	13	14	15	16	17	18	IN
472	408	417	216	508	469	612	150	467	3719
4	4	4	3	5	4	5	3	4	36

SAN FRANCISCO GOLF CLUB — PAR: 71 YARDAGE: 6716

1	2	3	4	5	6	7	8	9	OUT
523	424	388	220	381	422	190	378	582	3508
5	4	4	3	4	4	3	4	5	36

10	11	12	13	14	15	16	17	18	IN
410	161	408	381	344	169	375	430	530	3208
4	3	4	4	4	3	4	4	5	35

SCIOTO COUNTRY CLUB — PAR: 71 YARDAGE: 6950

1	2	3	4	5	6	7	8	9	OUT
418	459	381	188	439	527	378	509	160	3459
4	4	4	3	4	5	4	5	3	36

10	11	12	13	14	15	16	17	18	IN
421	360	546	446	236	425	420	191	446	3491
4	4	5	4	3	4	4	3	4	35

THE COUNTRY CLUB (COMPOSITE) — PAR: 71 YARDAGE: 7033

1	2	3	4	5	6	7	8	9	OUT
450	190	451	335	432	310	197	378	513	3256
4	4	4	4	4	4	3	4	4	35

10	11	12	13	14	15	16	17	18	IN
447	450	486	436	534	432	186	370	436	3777
4	5	3	4	5	4	3	4	4	35

SEMINOLE GOLF CLUB — PAR: 72 YARDAGE: 6787

1	2	3	4	5	6	7	8	9	OUT
370	387	501	450	202	383	432	235	494	3454
4	4	5	4	3	4	4	3	5	36

10	11	12	13	14	15	16	17	18	IN
382	420	367	168	499	495	410	175	417	3333
4	4	4	3	5	5	4	3	4	36

THE GOLF CLUB — PAR: 72 YARDAGE: 7268

1	2	3	4	5	6	7	8	9	OUT
372	444	185	594	453	470	528	135	409	3590
4	4	3	5	4	4	5	3	4	36

10	11	12	13	14	15	16	17	18	IN
383	183	456	369	618	449	200	553	467	3678
4	3	4	4	5	4	3	5	4	36

SHADOW CREEK — PAR: 72 YARDAGE: 7239

1	2	3	4	5	6	7	8	9	OUT
404	401	443	553	206	476	567	181	409	3640
4	4	4	5	3	4	5	3	4	36

10	11	12	13	14	15	16	17	18	IN
426	327	395	232	473	438	617	164	527	3599
4	4	4	3	4	4	5	3	5	36

THE OLYMPIC CLUB (LAKE) — PAR: 71 YARDAGE: 6842

1	2	3	4	5	6	7	8	9	OUT
533	394	223	438	457	439	288	137	433	3342
5	4	3	4	4	4	4	3	4	35

10	11	12	13	14	15	16	17	18	IN
422	430	410	186	417	157	609	522	347	3500
4	4	4	3	4	3	5	5	4	36

SHINNECOCK HILLS GOLF CLUB — PAR: 70 YARDAGE: 6944

1	2	3	4	5	6	7	8	9	OUT
394	226	453	408	535	471	188	367	447	3489
4	3	4	4	5	4	3	4	4	35

10	11	12	13	14	15	16	17	18	IN
409	158	472	377	444	415	544	186	450	3455
4	3	4	4	4	4	5	3	4	35

TPC AT SAWGRASS (STADIUM) — PAR: 72 YARDAGE: 6954

1	2	3	4	5	6	7	8	9	OUT
388	520	162	380	454	381	439	215	582	3521
4	5	3	4	4	4	4	3	5	36

10	11	12	13	14	15	16	17	18	IN
415	529	353	172	455	440	497	132	440	3433
4	5	4	3	4	4	5	3	4	36

SOUTHERN HILLS COUNTRY CLUB — PAR: 71 YARDAGE: 7014

1	2	3	4	5	6	7	8	9	OUT
460	471	405	372	655	178	384	228	374	3527
4	4	4	4	5	3	4	3	4	35

10	11	12	13	14	15	16	17	18	IN
396	173	458	537	223	413	491	358	465	3487
4	3	4	5	3	4	5	4	4	36

WANNAMOISETT COUNTRY CLUB — PAR: 69 YARDAGE: 6661

1	2	3	4	5	6	7	8	9	OUT
428	474	138	445	379	429	347	183	443	3266
4	4	3	4	4	4	4	3	4	34

10	11	12	13	14	15	16	17	18	IN
416	393	215	383	368	200	429	545	446	3395
4	4	3	4	4	3	4	5	4	35

SPYGLASS HILL GOLF COURSE — PAR: 72 YARDAGE: 6862

1	2	3	4	5	6	7	8	9	OUT
595	349	152	370	183	416	529	399	431	3424
5	4	3	4	3	4	5	4	4	36

10	11	12	13	14	15	16	17	18	IN
407	528	178	445	560	125	464	325	408	3438
4	5	3	4	5	3	4	4	4	36

WINGED FOOT GOLF CLUB (WEST) — PAR: 72 YARDAGE: 6956

1	2	3	4	5	6	7	8	9	OUT
446	411	216	453	515	324	166	442	471	3444
4	4	3	4	5	4	3	4	5	36

10	11	12	13	14	15	16	17	18	IN
190	386	535	212	418	417	457	449	448	3512
3	4	5	3	4	4	5	4	4	36

THE CASCADES — PAR: 70 YARDAGE: 6679

1	2	3	4	5	6	7	8	9	OUT
398	432	289	210	575	367	417	153	448	3289
4	4	4	3	5	4	4	3	4	35

10	11	12	13	14	15	16	17	18	IN
381	192	476	440	429	229	527	513	203	3390
4	3	4	4	4	3	5	5	3	35

Index

Author's Dedication

For Dad, who showed me;

For Mom, who listened;

For Annie Kate and Jack, who just make me smile;

For Kathy, who does it all.

Author's Acknowledgements

All books are collaborative efforts. This one is no exception. There are a frightening array of contributory documents, books and stories that made the research of this volume possible, if not tolerable. Even before I started on this book, my understanding of golf course architecture was fueled by Ron Whitten, Golf Digest's senior editor. Having Ron's unequalled expertise and guidance at the start (and particularly at the finish) of this project helped shape it and keep it on track. Moreover, his book with Geoffrey Cornish, *The Architects of Golf*, is not only the definitive history and sourcebook of the art of golf course architecture, but an engaging read as well.

There are other important books that provided glimpses of the great golf courses. In particular, there is *The World Atlas of Golf*, Bradley Klein's important work *Discovering Donald Ross*, *The Life and Work of Dr. Alister Mackenzie*, the collection of Donald Ross memoirs *Golf Has Never Failed Me* and Robert Trent Jones Sr.'s volume *Golf's Magnificent Challenge*. There have been the assorted wonderful individual club histories, particularly those produced for Colonial Country Club, Garden City Golf Club, Prairie Dunes Golf Club, Riviera and The Golf Club. One other source of interesting commentary and description was found at the website *www.golfclubatlas.com*, where the palpable enthusiasm for golf course design is inspiring for both neophyte and veteran architecture enthusiast.

A special thanks goes to Luke Friend and the rest of the people at Carlton Publishing for shepherding this book from initial concept to final design.

In addition, there have been many individuals who were of great assistance. First, there would be no book without the tremendous talent of principally Stephen Szurlej and others like Jim Moriarty and Tony Roberts, whose photography deservedly takes center stage in these pages. Tom Emanuel, Leslie Armstrong and Julie Ware in the Golf Digest Licensing Department were unfailingly upbeat and efficient during trying deadlines. Cliff Schrock helped unearth more than one long lost historical tournament program from the files of the Golf Digest Resource Center. Melissa Yow volunteered her keen eye and attention to detail at the end when it really mattered.

Finally and most importantly, I cannot say how much I owe to my wife and family. Annie Kate and Jack have waited too long for Daddy to come home and play, and no one contributed more to the writing of this book than my wife Kathy, who has consoled, corrected and counseled all in the right measure and all at the right time.

She made it possible on a daily basis for this book to happen.

Picture Credits

Associated Press/Wide World: 91t; 99t; 115t; 155t

Bay Hill Golf Club: 27b

R. Beckwith: 55t; 215t

Crystal Downs Country Club Archives: 46b

East Lake Golf Club: 56-57; 58-59; 59b

Bob Ewell: 195t

Bill Fields: 139t; 206b

David Fleurant/Light Impression: 208-209; 210-211; 211b

Golf Digest Archives: 23t; 43t; 59t; 71t; 107t; 131t; 163t

Golf World Photos: 127t; 167t; 199t; 203t; 211t

International News Photos: 87t

Klemme/Golfoto: 147b

Rusty Jarrett: 207

E.D. Lacey: 75t

Larry Lambrecht Photography: 67b

Lawrence Levy: 143t

Los Angeles Country Club: 84-85; 86b; 86-87

Jim Moriarty: 2-3; 14-15; 51b; 72-73; 74-75; 75b; 79t; 80-81; 82-83; 83b; 91b; 95t; 108-109; 128-129; 131b; 134b; 139b; 140-141; 142b; 142-143; 172-173; 174b; 174-175; 175t; 188-189; 190; 190-191; 206-207; 212-213

Lester Nehamkin: 123t

Pacific & Atlantic Photos, Inc.: 39t

Denis Roberson: 43b

© Tony Roberts Photography: 52-53; 54b; 54-55; 62b; 90-91; 120-121; 120-121; 122-123; 123b; 162-163; 163b; 187b

Stephen Szurlej: 1; 4-5; 6-7; 8-9; 10-11; 12-13; 16-17; 18-19; 19t; 19b; 20-21; 22b; 22-23; 24-25; 26-27; 27t; 28-29; 30b; 30-31; 32-33; 34-35; 35b; 35t; 36-37; 38b; 38-39; 40-41; 42-43; 44-45; 46-47; 48-49; 50-51; 51t; 60-61; 62-63; 63t; 64-65; 66-67; 68-69; 70-71; 76-77; 78b; 78-79; 83t; 88-89; 92-93; 94b; 94-95; 96-97; 98-99; 99b; 100-101; 102b; 102-103; 103t; 104-105; 106-107; 107b; 110b; 110-111; 111t; 112-113; 114-115; 115b; 116-117; 118b; 118-119; 124-125; 126b; 126-127; 132-133; 134-135; 135t; 136-137; 138-139; 144-145; 146-147; 147t; 148-149; 150b; 150-151; 151t; 156-157; 158b; 158-159; 159t; 160-161; 164-165; 166b; 166-167; 168-169; 170-171; 171b; 176-177; 178-179; 179t; 179b; 180-181; 182b; 182-183; 183t; 184-185; 186-187; 187t; 187bl; 192-193; 194-195; 195b; 196-197; 198b; 198-199; 200-201; 202-203; 203b; 204-205; 214b; 214-215; 216

United Press International: 31t; 119t

© USGA: 47t; 67t; 191t. **By John Mummert:** 70b; 152-153; 154-155; 155b

Ron Whitten: 130-131

Wilson Sportpix: 171t